Knowledge and Reasoning for Answering Questions 2011

(KRAQ 2011)

Held at the 5th International Joint Conference on Natural Language Processing 2011 (IJCNLP 2011)

Chiang Mai, Thailand
12 November 2011

ISBN: 978-1-62276-442-6

Printed from e-media with permission by:

Curran Associates, Inc.
57 Morehouse Lane
Red Hook, NY 12571

CURRAN ASSOCIATES INC.
proceedings
.com

Some format issues inherent in the e-media version may also appear in this print version.

Printed by Curran Associates, Inc. (2012)

Association for Computational Linguistics
209 N. Eighth Street
Stroudsburg, Pennsylvania 18360

Phone: 1-570-476-8006
Fax: 1-570-476-0860

acl@aclweb.org

Additional copies of this publication are available from:

Curran Associates, Inc.
57 Morehouse Lane
Red Hook, NY 12571 USA
Phone: 845-758-0400
Fax: 845-758-2634
Email: curran@proceedings.com
Web: www.proceedings.com

TABLE OF CONTENTS

Introduction

The introduction of reasoning capabilities in question-answering (QA) systems appeared in the late 70s. A second generation of QA systems, aimed at being cooperative, emerged in the late 80s - early 90s. In these systems, quite advanced reasoning models were developed on closed domains to go beyond the production of direct responses to a query, in particular when the query has no response or when it contains misconceptions. More recently, systems such as JAVELIN, Inference WEB or Cogex, operating over open domains, gradually integrated inferential components, but not as advanced as those of the 90s. The performances of state-of-the-art systems such as the above (as highlighted e.g. in recent TREC-QA tracks) show that reasoning components substantially improve the response relevance and accuracy. Thcy can also potentially be much more cooperative.

On the one hand, there is still a long way before being able to produce accurate, cooperative and robust QA systems, because of the very large complexity of natural systems and of the need to make several communities work together on common grounds.

On the other hand, recent foundational, methodological and technological developments in knowledge representation (e.g. ontologies, knowledge bases incorporating various forms of incompleteness or uncertainty), in speech processing, in multimedia and multimodality, and in advanced language processing resources and techniques (for question processing as well as for generating responses) make it possible to foresee the elaboration of much more accurate, cooperative and robust systems dedicated to answering questions from multimedia supports or from textual data, from e.g. online texts or web pages, operating either on open or closed domains.

The user interface aspects regarding both input and output (e.g. SMS or advanced interfaces, on line help, dialogue, etc.) and their integration into interactive environments are also crucial for the viability of such systems.

We thank all authors who submitted papers. The review process was implemented in a way such that papers conform to the IJCNLP objectives and level. We thanks the important work made by our reviewers.

Patrick Saint-Dizier

Organizers:

Patrick Saint-Dizier (main contact), IRIT, France,
Philippe Blache, LPL, Aix, France,
Asanee Kawtrakul, Kasetsart University, Bangkok,
Alisa Kongthon, NECTEC, Thailand,
Marie-Francine Moens , KUL, Belgium,
Silvia Quarteroni, Politecnico Milano, Italy.

Program Committee:

Sivaji Bandyopadhyay, Jadavpur Univ. Kolkata, India,
Hutchatai Chanlekha, Kasetsart Univ., Bangkok, Thailand,
Meritxell Gonzalez, UPC, Barcelona, Spain
Marco Dinarelli, LIMSI, Paris, France
Rachel Edita Roxas, DLSU , Manilla, The Philippines,
Sophie Rosset LIMSI, France,
Chai Wutiwiwatchai, The Director of Human Language Technology Laboratory of NECTEC, Thailand.

Invited Speakers:

Silvia Quarteroni,
Alisa Kongthon,
Philippe Blache.

We wish to thank our sponsors

Gold Sponsors

www.google.com

www.baidu.com

The Office of Naval Research (ONR)

The Asian Office of Aerospace Research and Development (AOARD)

Department of Systems Engineering and Engineering Managment, The Chinese University of Hong Kong

Silver Sponsors

Microsoft Corporation

Bronze Sponsors

Chinese and Oriental Languages Information Processing Society (COLIPS)

Supporter

Thailand Convention and Exhibition Bureau (TCEB)

We wish to thank our sponsors

Organizers

Asian Federation of Natural Language Processing (AFNLP)

National Electronics and Computer Technology Center (NECTEC), Thailand

Sirindhorn International Institute of Technology (SIIT), Thailand

Rajamangala University of Technology Lanna (RMUTL), Thailand

Maejo University, Thailand

Chiang Mai University (CMU), Thailand

The KOMODO System: getting Recommendations on how to realize an action via Question-Answering

Marc Canitrot, Thomas de Filippo, Pierre-Yves Roger
Prometil
42 Avenue du Gal Decroute
31100 Toulouse, France
m.canitrot@prometil.com

Patrick Saint-Dizier
IRIT-CNRS, 118, route de Narbonne
31062 Toulouse cedex France
stdizier@irit.fr

Abstract

In this paper, we present the KOMODO system which is designed to provide tips (advice and warnings) on the way to realize a task from user queries. Information is extracted from web services. We present the different steps of the system: web page selection, ranking and cleaning, extraction of warnings and advice, relevance analysis and contextualization, and production of a response. The different language processing steps are presented together with an evaluation of the results. The system is fully tested and a demonstration will be made if possible during the presentation.

1 Introduction

Given a few key-words, such as *put up wall paper*, Komodo is more than a question-answering system: it provides a series of recommendations or hints to realize this task. these are given under the form of advice and warnings, together with a few explanations. These recommendations are extracted from various web pages which are in general procedures describing how to realize that task, selected as relevant and reliable. Therefore, Komodo explains how to do something, but it offers more by compiling advice and warnings from various candidate pages.

Getting advice, hints and warnings is of much importance for different types of unexperimented users who have a task to realize but want to know more about it before really starting. Obviously, it is often possible to find a web page that explains, on the basis of a procedure, how to realize this task. However, quite frequently, these are not so rich in recommendations, they basically describe the different steps of the work under the form of instructions to follow. Psychological experiments have in fact shown that, besides instructions given in procedures, users are very much interested in what remains implicit in those texts: what you are supposed to know or care about, but have no means to ask or to guess. Komodo is aimed to fill in this kind of gap.

Procedures are designed to guide people step by step to realize precise tasks (Delin et ali. 1994) (Takechi et ali. 2003). They consist of a sequence of instructions, designed with some accuracy in order to reach a goal (e.g. assemble a computer). Procedural texts may also include subgoals. These are most of the time realized by means of titles and subtitles. The user must carefully follow step by step the given instructions in order to reach the goal (Rosner et ali. 1992). The How-to question answering aspect was developed in (Yin 2004), Aouladomar et al. 2005) and (Delpech et al. 2008).

Procedures abound in a number of domains, from apparently simple cooking recipes to large maintenance manuals. They include documents as diverse as teaching texts, medical notices, social behavior recommendations, directions for use, assembly notices, do-it-yourself notices, itinerary guides, savoir-faire guides etc. (Aouladomar et al., 2005). Procedural texts follow a number of structural criteria, whose realization may depend on the author's writing abilities, on the targeted user, and on traditions associated with a given domain. Procedural texts can be regulatory, procedural, programmatory, prescriptive or injunctive.

We have developed a quite detailed analysis of procedural texts, identifying their main basic components as well as their global structure. Procedural texts are complex structures, they often exhibit a quite complex rational (the instructions) and 'irrational' structure which is mainly composed of advices, conditions, preferences, evaluations, user stimulations, etc. They form what is called the explanation structure, which motivates and justifies the goal-instructions structure, which is the backbone of procedural texts. A number of these elements are forms of argumentation, they provide a strong and essential internal cohesion and coherence to procedural texts (Anscombre et al. 1981).

An important aspect of this project at a cognitive level is the accurate identification of the explanation structure as found in procedural texts in order (1) to better understand explanation strategies deployed by humans in precise, concrete and operational situations (VanderLinden 1003) and (2) then to be able to provide a set recommendations that would guide users when the perform a task, more or less independently of the precise procedure they follow.

We have already studied the instructional aspects of procedural texts and implemented quite an efficient prototype within the <TextCoop> project that tags texts with dedicated XML tags. The Dislog language (Discourse in Logic) allows the specification of rules that describe the various forms discourse structures can take (Anonymous 2011). In this paper, after a general presentation of the explanation structure in procedures, we focus on the form warnings and advice take in procedures and how these can be extracted using Dislog. We then survey the main steps of the Komodo system from the query to the production of a series of recommendations (advice and warnings) meant to inform a user who wants to realize a certain taks. The Komodo system is now operational, if accepted a demo will be given during the talk. At this moment, it basically works for French, a transposition to English is planned. Some elements of procedural text processing, in particular various forms of explanations have been also tested for Thai.

2 The explanation structure in procedural texts

We first present, in this section, the general organization of the explanation structure as it emerged from corpus analysis.

From our development corpus (1700 web texts of 1 to 3 pages of raw text from 24 different domains, large public and professional), we established a classification of the different forms explanations may take. Basically, the explanation structure is meant to guide the user in two ways: (1) by making sure that he will effectively realize actions as they are specified, via arguments (Amgoud et ali. 2005), (Amgoud et ali. 2001)) such as threats, rewards, advices and warnings which are 'coercitive' in a certain sense, and (2) help considerations such as evaluation of work realized so far and encouragements of different kinds.

Basically, the explanation structure is meant to guide the user by making sure that he will effectively realize actions as they are specified, via e.g. threats, rewards, evaluations, advices and warnings (Moschler 1985) (Bourse et al 2011). This structure has a strong causal structure (Talmy 2001). The main structures are facilitation and argumentation structures; they are either global (they are adjoined to goals, and have scope over the whole procedure) or local, included into instructional compounds. These structures are summarized as follows (the terms we use are either borrowed from works on rhetorical relations or are just ours if none exist):

- **facilitation structures**, which are rhetorical in essence (Kosseim et al 2000) (Van der Linden 1993), correspond to *How to do X ?* questions, these include two subcategories:
  (1) user help, with: hints, evaluations and encouragements and
  (2) controls on instruction realization, with two cases: (2.1) controls on actions: guidance, focusing, expected result and elaboration and (2.2) controls on user interpretations: definitions, reformulations, illustrations and also elaborations.

- **argumentation structures**, corresponding to *why do X ?* questions. These have either:
  (1) a positive orientation with the author involvement (promises) or not (advices and justifications) or
  (2) a negative orientation with the author involvement (threats) or not (warnings).

In what follows, we will mainly concentrate on this second point, and in particular on warnings and advices which are the most frequently encountered (since there are rarely involvements from the author). These will be used to construct the know-how knowledge base. Roughly, we have about 25% of instructions which have recommendations in do-it-yourself texts, and up to 60% in social procedural texts. Argumentation structures are relatively general to an applications domain, while facilitation structures are much more specific to the text and the targeted audiences.

Explanations and arguments help the user understand why an instruction must be realized and what are the risks or the drawbacks if he does not do it properly. The following example is typical of what is usually found:

[$_{instructional\ compound}$
[$_{Goal}$ To clean leather armchairs,]
[$_{argument:advice}$
[$_{instruction}$ choose specialized products dedicated to furniture,
[$_{instruction}$ and prefer them colorless]],
[$_{advicesupport}$ they will play a protection role, add beauty, and repair some small damages.]]]

We have here an argument of type advice which is composed of 2 instructions (later called a conclusion) and a conjunction of three supports which motivate the 2 instructions.

3 Identifying arguments in procedures

Argument detection and analysis has been developed in the <TextCoop> project and presented in previous papers. Lets us summarize the main results here for the sake of understanding.

3.1 Processing warnings

Warnings are basically organized around a unique structure composed of an 'avoid expression' combined with a proposition. The variations around the 'avoid expressions' capture the illocutionary force of the argument via several devices, ordered here by increasing force :
(1) 'prevention verbs like avoid' NP / to VP (*avoid hot water*)
(2) do not / never / ... VP(infinitive) ... (*never put this cloth in the sun*)
(3) it is essential, vital, ... to never VP(infinitive).
In cases where the conclusion is relatively weak in terms of consequences, it may not have any specific mark, its recognition is then based on the observation that it is the instruction that immediately precedes an already identified support.

Supports are propositions which are identified from various marks:
(1) via connectors such as: *sinon, car, sous peine de, au risque de* (otherwise, under the risk of), etc. or via verbs expressing consequence,
(2) via negative expressions of the form: *in order not to, in order to avoid, etc.*
(3) via specific verbs such as risk verbs introducing an event (*you risk to break*). In general the embedded verb has a negative polarity.
(4) via the presence of very negative terms, such as: nouns: *death, disease, etc.*, adjectives, and some verbs and adverbs. We have a lexicon of about 200 negative terms found in our corpora.

Some supports have a more neutral formulation: they may be a portion of a sentence where a conclusion has been identified. For example, a proposition in the future tense or conditional following a conclusion is identified as a support. However, as will be seen below, some supports may be empty, because they can easily be inferred by the reader. In that case, the argument is said to be truncated.

Patterns are implemented in Perl and are included into the TextCoop software. From the above observations, with some generalizations and the construction of lexicons of marks, we have summarized the extraction process in only 8 patterns for supports and 3 patterns for conclusions. In procedural texts, arguments are tagged by XML tags. We carried out an indicative evaluation (e.g. to get improvement directions) on a corpus of 66 texts over various domains, containing 262 arguments. We get the following results for warnings:

conclusion recognition	support recognition	(3)	(4)
88%	91%	95%	95%

(3) conclusions well delimited (4) supports well delimited, with respect to warnings correctly identified.

3.2 Processing Advice

Conclusions of type advice are identified essentially by means of two types of patterns (in French):
(1) advice or preference expressions followed by an instruction. The expressions may be a verb or a more complex expression: *is advised to, prefer, it is better, preferable to, etc.*,
(2) expression of optionality or of preference followed by an instruction: *our suggestions: ...*, or expression of optionality within the instruction (*use preferably a sharp knife*).
In addition, as for warnings, any instruction preceeding a support of type advice is a conclusion.

Supports of type advice are identified on the basis of 3 distinct types of patterns:
(1) Goal exp + (adverb) + positively oriented term. Goal expressions are e.g.: in order to, for, whereas adverb includes: better (in French: mieux, plus, davantage), and positively oriented term includes: nouns (savings, perfection, gain, etc.), adjectives

(efficient, easy, useful, etc.), or adverbs (well, simply, etc.). For this latter class of positively oriented terms we constructed a lexicon that contains about 50 terms. terms.
(2) goal expression with a positive consequence verb (favor, encourage, save, etc.), or a facilitation verb (improve, optimize, facilitate, embellish, help, contribute, etc.),
(3) the goal expression in (1) and (2) above can be replaced by the verb 'to be' in the future: *it will be easier to locate your keys*.

Similarly as above, we carried out an indicative evaluation on the same corpus of 66 texts containing 240 manually identified advices. We get the following results for advices:

conclusion recognition	support recognition	(3)	(4)	(5)
79%	84%	92%	91%	91%

(3) conclusions well delimited, (4) supports well delimited, both with respect to advices correctly identified. (5) support and conclusion correctly related.

The structures of English are quite similar. A short example of an annotated text is given in Fig. 1 below.

4 Constructing an repository of advice and warning for a task: capturing the domain know-how

Besides studying the textual structure of procedural texts and responding to How-to questions from the analysis of these texts, a major challenge of this work is the construction of a **domain know-how knowledge base**, which is probably quite basic, but which could be subject to interesting generalizations. This domain know-how is essentially composed of recommendations under the form of advice and warnings related to the execution of the task at stake, possibly coupled with a few additional explanations (e.g. illustrations, reformulations, etc.)

There are repositories of advice organized by sector of activity available on the Web (e.g. http://www.conseils-gratuit.com). These are realized manually: most of these advice come from hints sent by readers of these pages. These repositories contain in general simple advice and also small procedures which are hints to better realize a certain task. Automatically constructing such repositories is of much interest but also a major challenge in advanced question-answering. We will focus here on textual information, but it is clear that images and possibly videos should complement the text.

Let us now present the different steps of the task.

4.1 Overview of the main steps

The main steps are:

- getting the user query and submitting it to a search engine (Exalead in our case),
- processing the returned links: elimination of irrelevant links, ads, etc.
- downloading the first 50 pages returned by Exalead which have not been filtered out at the previous stage,
- sorting the returned pages by decreasing procedural quality in order to eliminate ill-formed pages, ads, poorly realized pages, etc., approximately the 20 first ones are kept. This decision is based on a relevance metrics we have elaborated.
- cleaning those 20 web pages: keeping only the textual information and some typography elements,
- parsing these pages at discourse level using the <TextCoop> system, the result is an XML tagging of the instructional aspects, prerequisites, advice and warnings based on the patterns given above and a few explanation forms.
- in order to get the best and the most relevant advice and warnings, only advice and warnings from the 'best' paragraphs (according to our relevance metrics) are extracted possibly with their context.
- construction of a response web page and a know-how repository (query - set of related advice and warnings) for future similar queries.

The following domains have been investigated and are addressed in the Komodo system: house, cooking, garden, computer, do it yourself, animals, beauty. In the next subsections the above steps are developed, in particular those related to language processing and question-answering. The

$[_{procedure}$
$[_{title}$ How to embellish your balcony
$[_{Prerequisites}$ 1 lattice, window boxes, etc.]
....
$[_{instructional-compound}$ In order to train a plant to grow up a wall, select first a sunny area, clean the floor and make sure it is flat......
$[_{Argument}$ $[_{Conclusion:Advice}$ You should better let a 10 cm interval between the wall and the lattice.]
$[_{Support:Advice}$ This space will allow the air to move around, which is beneficial for the health of your plant.]
......]]]]

Figure 1: An annotated procedure

work has been realized on French: English glosses are given here for the sake of readability. The investigations reported below have been realized from a development corpus of 1700 procedural texts, from 24 different domains.

The kernel of the system, <TextCoop> and the language resources are realized in SWI Prolog. Interfaces, web page collection and result construction are realized in Java, returned pages are processed 'in parallel' via a multithread implementation to enhance efficiency.

4.2 Downloading relevant procedural texts

The user query, which refers to a task to be realized, is submitted to the Exalead search engine, which handles query enrichment if needed. Contrary to Google, Exalead returns links which directly points to web pages. These links are analyzed in order to keep only those which correspond to professional sites. Redundant addresses are also eliminated. This first step of filtering does depend on the domain. For do-it-yourself, it is easy to access the main platforms that explain how to realize an action. This is not so easy e.g. for social recommendations where blogs are the richest sources in terms of advice. In this latter case, a list of 'hot' links is construcxted and constantly updated.

A total of 50 links are kept after this first filtering. Then, those pages which are directly refered to by these links are downloaded in parallel in order to limit loading delays.

These pages are then 'cleaned'. By this term, we mean keeping only the elements which are useful for our purpose: the text and a limited number of typographic marks. Our cleaning programme has a set of parameters that describe the typographic symbols (and possibly their context) that we wish to keep. The others are eliminated. This operations is crucial to eliminate ads, summaries, etc. We also have a list of 'stop-terms' which provoke the elimination of the sentence in which they occur (e.g. click here to get a free coupon). This process eliminates in general between 20 and 60page contents.

The next step aims at identifying among those 50 pages those which are really procedural. Indeed a number of these pages often turn out to be of little or no interest. In addition, texts which are really short (less than 80 words) are excluded a priori: it is unlikely that they contain any advice or warnings. From the inspection of 280 texts in our corpus, we defined a simple metrics that can detect the procedural level of of a text. This metrics has been elaborated by contrasting regular texts with procedural ones. Procedural texts are much richer in terms of action verbs, in the infinitive or imperative form (these are morphologically different in French). They also have a large number of typographic which is not often encountered in regular texts:

mark	procedure	regular text
action verbs	85%	52%
imperative forms	44%	17%
infinitive forms	40%	25%
typographic marks	17%	2%

Verb ratios are computed as follows: number of imperative verbs w.r.t. total number of verbs found. Typographic marks rate: number of marks w.r.t. total number of words in the text. Html marks count for one mark per html tag.

As can be seen the contrast is quite high between regular and procedural texts. Furthermore, we are interested in collecting the best texts, i.e. those with a rich typographic mark, with very standard verb forms in imperative or infrnitive forms. We can then use this metrics to sort those texts considering the most procedural ones first. The metrics is defined as follows:
$rate = NV/TV + 2x(TM/NW)$.
where NV is the total number of verbs in the imperative or infinitive form, TV is the total number

of verbs found in the text. TM is the total number of typographic marks found (which are related to procedures) and NW is the total number of words in the text. To have a better taking into account of the importance of typography, a weight of 2 is introduced for that parameter. This metrics is very simple, but seems to be sufficient for the task at stake.

Analysing the results of applying the metrics to gardening, do-it-yourself, health care and cooking, we get the following results:

text rank	metrics ratio	evaluation
1-5	> 0.80	highly procedural
6 - 10	0.80 to 0.70	very procedural
10-15	0.69 to 0.65	good
15-20	0.64 to 0.62	good
20-30	0.61 to 0.54	average

It seems therefore that a threshold of 0.62 for a text would guarantee that the text considered is of a good procedural quality. In the above experiment, this means keeping about 20 texts, but this number may be higher or smaller depending on the query and the domain.

4.3 Processing relevant procedures with <TextCoop>

Our aim is to provide users with relevant advice and warnings related to their query. In fact, a closer look at the selected procedural texts shows that they indeed contain warnings and advice but a number of of them turn out to be irrelevant w.r.t. the user query. For example, a text may contain an introduction with general purpose advice. Providing these advice in the response would mean some analysis and sorting work for the reader which may not feel so confident about the overall result.

The relevant advice and warnings are all in the text sections or paragraphs which indeed describe the actions to undertake to realize the procedure. To select these text portions, we use another simple metrics that computes the number of verb domains w.r.t. the total number of words. Text portions above a certain threshold (which is a domain dependent parameter) are kept and processed by <TextCoop>. The set of verbs typical of the domain is constructed via the analysis of quite a large number of procedures in that domain. The number of verbs associated with a domain turn out to be much higher than expected. For the gardening domain, we identified about 500 verbs, which is very high. To get this set of verbs, about 1250 procedures have been inspected. This figure is very high considering the number of available texts in gardening in French. For the gardening domain, the threshold above which paragraphs are relevant for warnings and advice extraction is O.O5. In that domain relevant verb frequency ranges from O.O2 to O.20. The threshold of O.O5 allows the extraction of about 64% of the total text, which is a really efficient filtering.

These text portions are then submitted for discourse processing to <TextCoop>. This system identifies: titles and subtitles, prerequisites, instructions, illustrations, goal expressions and warnings and advice. Assuming that 20 texts are selected and keeping only the relevant paragraphs, between 1 and 7 warnings or advice are extracted by text, with an average of 3 per text. This means about 60 warnings or advice (almost in equal proportion) are extracted over the 20 texts.

This figure, however, varies greatly from a domain to another. For 20 texts, we have:

domain	nb of words	nb of A/W
DIY	1100	60
cooking	800	22
gardening	1450	54
health care	1950	38
computer	1550	33

nb of words is the total number of words of all the 20 procedures.

As can be seen, the DIY domain is very rich in advice and warnings, health care is very verbose and advice are not always very easy to identify. The computer domain is for specialists: it therefore contains less advice or warnings.

4.4 Response construction

At this stage, there are still three main problems to resolve:

- redundancy elimination: the best advice or warning extracted among those which are almost synonyms should be kept,
- contextualisation: quite frequently an advice or a warning cannot be understood in isolation: it is therefore necessary to introduce some form of contextual information, e.g. for an easy pronominal or event reference resolution,

- relevance: all advice and warnings are a priori relevant, however some are more crucial than others: sorting them by decreasing order of importance would be helpful for the user, in particular when ther eare many.

Redundancy elimination is a very difficult to resolve efficiently, since it requires a lot of domain knowledge, and lexical and textual inference to detect equivalent information. To resolve this difficulty, we organize warnings and advice per web page. In that case we have between one and 7 advicc or warning per page, which is not so much, and redundancy is less visible because it occurs over different pages. In fact, then, this redundancy may be useful as a way to insist e.g. on a precaution to take.

This approach of displaying the response per web page also avoids the crucial problem of sorting advice and warnings by decreasing importance. However, to be cooperative with the user, we evaluate the strength of those statements, via the analysis of adverbs and injunctive forms, as described in the patterns above, and display each advice or warning with a logo that indicates its importance a priori.

Finally, contextualization is dealt with as follows. Warnings and advice which do not contain any kind of reference are displayed alone. The others are displayed with the instruction that immediately precedes them. Our observations show that this adequately resolves the context problem in about 90% of the cases.

An example is given in a screenshot in fig 2 (last page of this document).

5 Conclusion

The work presented here describes the different stpes of the Komodo project, which is designed to provide users with a set of recommendations under the form of advice and warnings useful to know before starting any task, a priori described by a procedure.

The system is interactive (a demo will be given if accepted): from his query a user gets a series of recommendations and links to the relevant pages in case he wants to know more about them or access the whole procedure. The kernel of the system, <TextCoop> and the language resources are realized in SWI Prolog. Interfaces, web page collection and result construction are realized in Java, returned pages are processed 'in parallel' via a multithread implementation to enhance efficiency. In our still experimental version a query is fully processed in an average of 4 seconds, which is still a bit high. Collecting web pages takes about 1.5 seconds and linguistic processing about 2 seconds.

Pairs query - responses are stored a database, called know-how database. This is useful for frequently asked questions. However, to avoid having outdated data, a robot updates reponses regularly so that at least once a week each query has an updated set of recommendations.

Acknowledgements This work is supported by the French ANR project LELIE and by the Franco-Indian cooperation framework IFCPAR under ref. ICT 4200-1.

References

Amgoud, L., Parsons, S., Maudet, N., *Arguments, Dialogue, and Negotiation*, in: 14th European Conference on Artificial Intelligence, Berlin, 2001.

Anscombre, J.-Cl. Ducrot, O., *Interrogation et Argumentation*, in Langue francaise, no 52, L'interrogation, 5 - 22, 1981.

Aouladomar, F., Saint-dizier, P., *Towards Answering Procedural Questions*, Workshop KRAQ05, IJCAI05, Edinburgh, 2005.

Bourse, S., Saint-Dizier, P., The grammar of explanation structures in technical texts, Sintagma, vol. 27, 2011.

Cruse, A., *Lexical Semantics*, Cambridge Univ. Press, 1986.

Delpech, E., Saint-Dizier, P., Investigating the Structure of Procedural Texts for Answering How-to Questions, LREC 2008, Marrakech.

Davidson, D., *Actions, Reasons, and Causes*, Journal of Philosophy, 60, 1963

Delin, J., Hartley, A., Paris, C., Scott, D., Vander Linden, K., *Expressing Procedural Relationships in Multilingual Instructions*, Proceedings of the Seventh International Workshop on Natural Language Generation, pp. 61-70, Maine, USA, 1994.

Delpech, E., Murguia, E., Saint-Dizier, P., *A Two-Level Strategy for Parsing Procedural Texts*, VSST07, Marrakech, October 2007.

Delpech, E., Saint-Dizier, P., Investigating the Structure of Procedural Texts for Answering How-to Questions, LREC 2008, Marrakech.

Gardent, C., Discourse tree adjoining grammars, report nb. 89, Univ. Saarlandes, Saarbrucken, 1997.

Kosseim, L., Lapalme, G., *Choosing Rhetorical Structures to Plan Instructional Texts*, Computational Intelligence, Blackwell, Boston, 2000.

Moschler, J., *Argumentation et Conversation, Eléments pour une Analyse Pragmatique du Discours*, Hatier - Crédif, 1985.

Rosner, D., Stede, M., *Customizing RST for the Automatic Production of Technical Manuals*, in R. Dale, E. Hovy, D. Rosner and O. Stock eds., Aspects of Automated Natural Language Generation, Lecture Notes in Artificial Intelligence, pp. 199-214, Springler-Verlag, 1992.

Takechi, M., Tokunaga, T., Matsumoto, Y., Tanaka, H., *Feature Selection in Categorizing Procedural Expressions*, The Sixth International Workshop on Information Retrieval with Asian Languages (IRAL2003), pp.49-56, 2003.

Talmy, L., Towards a Cognitive Semantics, vol. 1 and 2, MIT Press, 2001.

Vander Linden, K., *Speaking of Actions Choosing Rhetorical Status and Grammatical Form in Instructional Text Generation* Thesis, University of Colorado, 1993.

Webber, B., D-LTAG: extending lexicalized TAGs to Discourse, Cognitive Science 28, pp. 751-779, Elsevier, 2004.

Yin, L., *Topic Analysis and Answering Procedural Questions*, Information Technology Research Institute Technical Report Series, ITRI-04-14, University of Brighton, UK, 2004.

Zuckerman, I., McConachy, R., Korb, K., Using Argumentation Startegies in Automatic Argument Generation, INLG 2000, Israel.

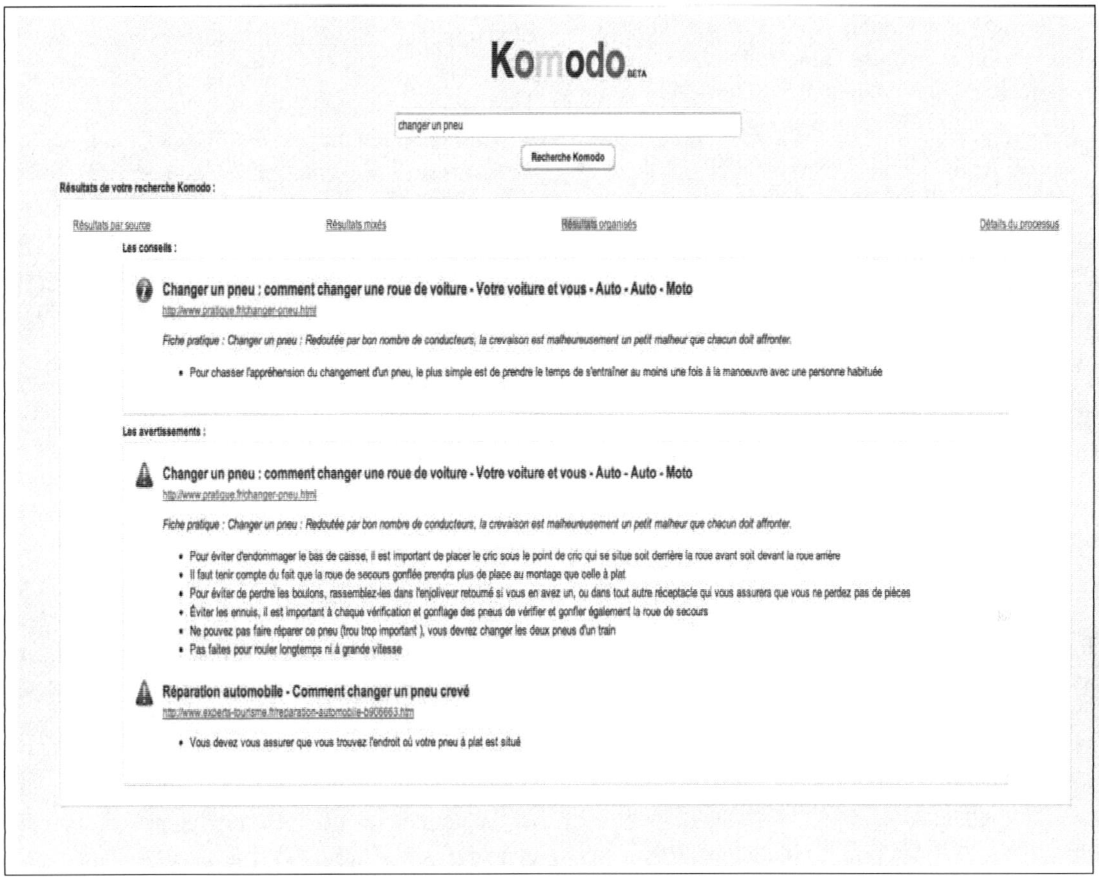

Figure 2: Screenshot of Komodo (experimental)

Question Answering, Semantic Search and Data Service Querying

Silvia Quarteroni
DEI - Politecnico di Milano
via Ponzio 34/5, 20133 Milan, Italy
quarteroni@elet.polimi.it

Abstract

Question Answering (QA) systems have profoundly evolved since their inception as natural language interfaces to databases. QA technology has indeed become state-of-the-art on open-domain, unstructured information retrieval and more recently touched the Semantic Web and the problem of querying structured data (e.g. RDF triples) on the Web. A natural new challenge is QA over data services, supporting simple natural language query interfaces to the composition of such services for extracting complex results. This paper discusses the above challenges and illustrates natural language QA over data services with a concrete example.

1 Introduction

Question Answering systems, originally designed as natural language interfaces to databases (Waltz, 1978), have nowadays evolved towards the open domain. This involves supporting natural language questions of arbitrary complexity (requiring e.g. definitions, explanations or complex factoids) and extracting answers from potentially unlimited data sources (Kwok et al., 2001).

Information Retrieval (IR) on unstructured data, e.g. Web documents and large textual collections, has been widely researched and is now a mature technology, partly thanks to evaluation campaigns such as TREC[1]. The same goes for QA systems, which are currently able to solve complex questions by exploiting search engines as their information retrieval modules (see e.g. (Moschitti and Quarteroni, 2010; Delpech and Saint-Dizier, 2008)).

On the other hand, recent work in the Semantic Web community has brought to the (semi-)automatic creation of semantic information from partially structured Web resources such as Wikipedia[2], resulting in wide-coverage knowledge bases like YAGO (Suchanek et al., 2007). This in turn has promoted the notion of *semantic search*, which may be defined as IR augmented with semantic information in the purpose of reasoning about the concepts involved in queries and answers (Fazzinga and Lukasiewicz, 2010). Also in the Semantic Web area, natural language interfaces to ontologies have been proposed in a number of studies as an alternative to keyword-based interfaces or interfaces based on query languages (Damljanovic et al., 2010b; Kaufmann and Bernstein, 2007). Generally speaking, NL interfaces to ontologies attempt to perform an exact mapping of the NL query into a logical formula in order to access knowledge structured in e.g. RDF triples.

Even more recently, the exponential growth of data providers on the Web has made proprietary data increasingly available through Web APIs, e.g. Google Places[3], and/or search-specific languages, e.g. the Yahoo Query Language[4]. Data sources are usually wrapped as data services, specified by input and output parameters; normally, the body of data services includes queries and the output is a data collection, with a structured or semi-structured schema.

Enabling natural language interfaces to data services is still an ambitious goal towards which there is little research; this paper analyze aspects of the above-mentioned technologies that bring this objective closer. It also illustrates ongoing work within the Search Computing project[5] that aims at accessing powerful result composition and ranking infrastructures via natural language multi-

[1] trec.nist.gov

[2] wikipedia.org

[3] code.google.com/apis/maps/documentation/places

[4] developer.yahoo.com/yql

[5] search-computing.it

domain questions.

The paper is organized as follows. Section 2 introduces a number of dimensions of question answering challenges; Section 3 discusses QA towards data services; Section 4 describes an approach towards natural language interfaces to data services. Finally, Section 5 illustrates a use case supporting natural language query processing and Section 6 concludes.

2 Questions: from documents to services

Table 1 reports a small snapshot of state-of-the-art information retrieval along two dimensions: query language (logical vs natural) and data sources (unstructured documents, ontologies and services). While querying unstructured documents in natural language offers challenges in terms of the difficulty of specific types of questions (e.g. definitions (Moschitti and Quarteroni, 2010) and procedures (Delpech and Saint-Dizier, 2008)) and the robustness/confidence of information extraction from text, ontologies and data services offer different types of issues. On the one hand, information is structured and may be retrieved with a high degree of confidence, however the main problems deal with interfacing with data sources, i.e. mapping the user's query into a logical format, and possible with executing such a query by composing different data services. Sections 2.1 and 2.2 deal in particular with the issues of performing QA over ontologies and data services.

2.1 Semantic Search

Question Answering over semantic information has been proposed in recent years (McGuinness, 2004) as a natural consequence of the development of Semantic Web technologies. QA is indeed agreed to be one of the ultimate objectives of Semantic Search (Fazzinga and Lukasiewicz, 2010), encouraged by the fact that a number of user studies have found natural language queries to be the most user-friendly and time-efficient input format to semantic information (Kaufmann and Bernstein, 2007; Damljanovic and Bontcheva, 2009). However, open domain QA on this type of resources is far from being a consolidated discipline, partly due to the gap between well-defined semantic resources as can be found for specific domains and the unstructured nature of Web information at large.

Another important issue is the nature of interaction with a semantic QA service, as performing the lexical to semantic level mapping needed to interpret natural language queries into combinations of domain concepts is an only partially solved problem. Typical approaches in this direction involve a combination of statistical techniques (syntactic parsing) and semantic operations to identify ontology concepts in the user's input. For instance, QUERIX (Kaufmann et al., 2006) combines the Stanford parser (Klein and Manning, 2003) with WordNet[6] to obtain RDF triples from natural language user queries, while PANTO (Wang et al., 2007) translates the syntactic parse tree of a natural language query into SPARQL by exploiting a reference lexicon. This often involves user interaction to support the system's interpretation, as in (Damljanovic et al., 2010b).

A crucial question is to figure out whether open domain QA techniques, which leverage statistical methods and require minimal (if any) intervention at design stage, can be successfully combined with semantic search techniques, in order to leverage the benefits of both. In this perspective, the development and widespread usage of vast knowledge bases such as DBPedia[7], GeoNames[8] and YAGO (Suchanek et al., 2007) demonstrates that semantics can encompass universal vocabularies and domains, opening the way to open-domain search.

2.2 Querying Data Services

Recent initiatives such as the W3C Linked Open Data[9] community project are fostering the adoption of Linked Data (LD) as a best practice. Clearly, the widespread presence of data services makes them a valuable resource for IR; however, the problems typically addressed in this field concern service discovery (Carenini et al., 2008), automatic composition (Martin et al., 2007; Fensel et al., 2011) and mediation (Manolescu et al., 2005) rather than the issue of interfacing to data services.

In particular, natural language interfaces are still at an early stage: for instance, (Lim and Lee, 2010) propose a mapping of natural language query blocks to services using predefined workflow templates, however it may be generally said that "core NLP" methods are still far from the data service querying problem. Section 3 reports

[6] wordnet.princeton.edu

[7] `www.dbpedia.org`

[8] `http://www.geonames.org/ontology`

[9] `esw.w3.org/SweoIG/TaskForces/CommunityProjects/LinkingOpenData`

Table 1: Querying documents, ontologies, services

Query Language	Documents	Ontologies	Data services
Logical	-	Semantic search (Fazzinga and Lukasiewicz, 2010)	LOD, YQL, OWL-S (Martin et al., 2007)
Natural	Open-domain QA (Moschitti and Quarteroni, 2010; Delpech and Saint-Dizier, 2008)	QUERIX (Kaufmann et al., 2006), PANTO (Wang et al., 2007), (Damljanovic et al., 2010b)	(Lim and Lee, 2010), SeCo (Bozzon et al., 2011b)

progress in the direction of open-domain QA over data services.

3 Towards QA over Data Services

In order to conduct QA over data services, the semantics of the latter needs to be aligned to the semantics of natural language interpretation; such a mapping should be carried out with minimal human contribution, maximal domain coverage, and a high level of robustness. Ideally, natural language interpretation of the user's question should map the user's intent (expected answer type in QA terminology) and the main concepts mentioned in the question to the same knowledge representation used by service interfaces to execute queries over their respective data services.

To this end, we have been working on a pragmatic approach to the description of data services in the SeCo project (Bozzon et al., 2011a), that aims at efficiently and effectively composing data services in order to address complex queries. Here, the infrastructure supports the efficient execution of queries over service compositions and different ranking schemes are also deployed for result presentation flexibility. The models used for service description and annotation in the purpose of querying are described in Section 3.1, while querying itself is described in Section 3.2.

3.1 Pragmatic Service Annotation

We model data services at different levels of abstraction according to a three level Service Description Framework (SDF). The topmost conceptual level, denoted as *service mart* level, represents the domain entities described by services (e.g. **Theater**).

Then, the logical view sees possible implementations of data services focused on specific entities in terms of *access patterns* (APs), i.e. relations between the I/O parameters they involve. For example, an AP returning movies shown near the user's current position would be named `GET Movie WITH Theater BY CurrentPosition`.

Finally, at the physical level, *service interfaces* encode the actual interaction protocol; different service interfaces may be associated to the same AP, e.g. a YQL service returning US movies based on the user's position or a wrapper to the Google movies service returning Italian movies and theaters by location. The above three views compose the so-called Service Description Framework (SDF).

Access Pattern information from data services is used for building a common *domain diagram* (DD), for which we use a simple Entity-Relationship model. Each data service is "focused" upon a DD entity, has a schema which includes several related entities, and is linked to other data services through relationships. Figure 1 illustrates a sample DD deriving from services dealing with movies and theaters.

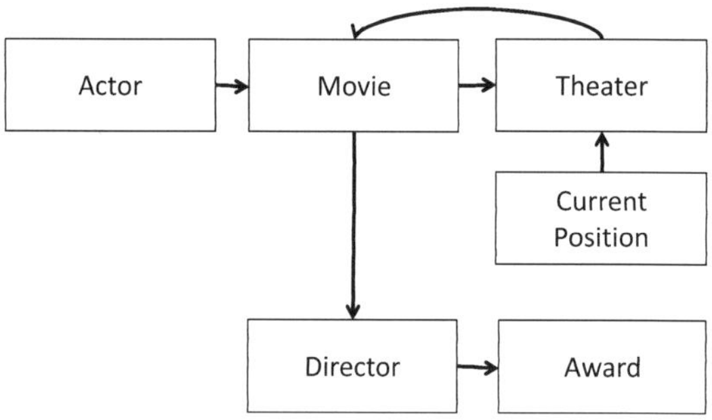

Figure 1: A sample Domain Diagram

One or more existing *knowledge bases* (KBs) are used as a reference for DD terminology and entities in order to validate it and support natural language querying; for instance, Section 4 shows an example of usage of YAGO (Suchanek et al., 2007) as the reference KB.

In addition to the DD, a *knowledge base proxy* (KBP) is constructed by using the reference KB to extract the most relevant concepts for describing the DD and reasoning upon those concepts.

The SDF is progressively populated in a bottom-up fashion by processing service interfaces available from data service providers and devising the corresponding APs by identifying the relevant DD entities they involve. In case no suitable entities are found in the DD, the reference KB is used as a source of entities that are immediately "projected" over the DD. Once access patterns are created and their focal entity is identified, the corresponding service mart is the one identified by such a focal entity.

3.2 Query Processing

Once available services have been registered following the method in Section 3.1, they can be queried in a variety of ways, including via Graphical User Interfaces or via textual input. In all cases, the general processing of a query over the registered data services is organized according to three steps, as summarized in Figure 2.

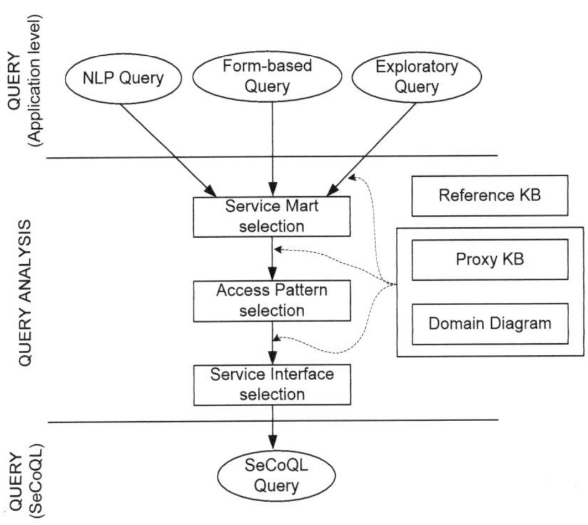

Figure 2: Top-down query processing steps over the Service Description Framework, with the contribution of domain semantics encoded in the Domain Diagram, the Knowledge Base Proxy and the reference Knowledge Base.

Starting from the queries submitted by the user in various formats at the application level, the steps progressively "formalize" the semantics of such queries at the conceptual, logical and physical level, mapping their terms into objects of the Service Description Framework. In brief, the core entities must be identified in the user's query in order to locate relevant service marts; once the latter are known, a suitable access pattern must be chosen for each service mart in order to fill in the query's input/output parameters; finally, a physical service implementation must be chosen to route the query to the appropriate data service.

As SeCo allows for the composition and concatenation of different data services, constraints must be formulated according to how APs are combined. These are expressed in a specific query format named SeCoQL (Braga et al., 2011), an SQL variation supporting queries over data services. A SeCoQL query is the final outcome of the query process in Figure 2.

Section 4 illustrates how a natural language query may be mapped to a logical query language expression invoking service interfaces and APs that refer to the Semantic Annotation Framework.

4 Natural Language Service Querying

Addressing a natural language (NL) query over the service registration architecture outlined in the previous section implies the difficulty of generalizing over text by mapping the lexical level to the conceptual representation of the domain at hand. We represent natural language query processing as a three-step process: first, a (probabilistic) matching is made between each query's syntactic focus and a focal DD entity connected to a service mart; then, a number of refinement operations allow to obtain the I/O parameters of APs; finally, AP parameters are mapped into lower-level service interface parameters to complete query specification. We summarize these steps as intent classification, access pattern selection and service interface selection, as described in the remainder of this section.

4.1 Step 1: Intent Classification

The processing of a natural language query starts with intent classification, i.e. a categorization of the user's query in terms of eligible service marts. Such a query categorization method must be able to decompose an arbitrarily complex, multi-domain query q into N subqueries q_i, $i \in \{1, .., N\}$. Then, it must map each q_i into a class c_j from the set of all query classes C, such that each c_j is mapped to a service mart in the conceptual model – or *other* to account for uninterpretable input.

Query decomposition can be performed in many ways; for instance, a method based on syntactic parsing will determine a sentence's subclauses as well as their syntactic relationships (coordination or subordination).

Once subqueries are identified, the next step

toward intent classification is the identification of the question's syntactic foci, i.e. its salient words/phrases, each of which is to be later matched to one of the available service marts. This is performed according to domain-independent criteria based on morphological and/or (shallow) syntactic analysis (Li et al., 2009; Damljanovic et al., 2010a). This process can be re-conducted to the question classification phase in open-domain Question Answering, which consists in estimating the most likely expected answer type from a domain-independent taxonomy – see e.g. (Li and Roth, 2002).

A pilot experiment To investigate intent classification, we ran a pilot experiment in question focus identification by comparing a number of existing focus extraction algorithms on a collection of 50 spontaneous user queries dealing with movies, theaters, lodgings and events, collected within the SeCo project. Queries in the collection have a single focus and do not require an initial decomposition, e.g. "where can I stay for one night close to cinema Plinius?". On the latter corpus, we have reached a recall of 69% when applying the state-of-the-art focus identification algorithm proposed by (Li et al., 2009). In addition, we were able to observe that, out of the 33 correctly identified foci, 14 could directly be mapped to a specific service mart (e.g. "movie", "events"); of the remaining queries, 5 referred to a synonym of a service mart identifier (e.g. "cinemas", a synonym of *Theater*), while 3 referred to subclasses of an identifier (e.g. "exhibition" is a type of *Event*). For all of the above cases, the presence of a KB indexing instances and preferred meanings of such terms has enabled the lexical to conceptual mapping. The 9 remaining foci referred to terms amenable to a specific service mart only after context disambiguation, e.g. "room" or "place", which both refer to the *Hotel* service mart; again, such context disambiguation is feasible by looking at KB properties of concepts around the focus entity.

This suggests that the accuracy of mapping foci to service marts is greatly dependent on both the precision of focus extraction and the ability to generalize and perform shallow reasoning abilities over the DD and KB; a machine learning approach may provide a more robust result than simple rule-based mapping in case a representative dataset is available.

4.2 Step 2: Access Pattern Selection

Once focal entities are identified, the subsequent step in NL query processing consists in selecting the AP that best responds to the user information needs for each focus. One possibility is to make a hypothesis about the best AP to represent the DD entities/attributes extracted so far from the user's query and then interacting with the user for obtaining the missing information. The best match with respect to the user's query is computed by selecting the AP that:

1. uses all the inputs provided by the user or by other outputs of previously selected APs;
2. requires the minimum number of additional inputs with respect to the ones provided by the user;
3. produces the maximum number of outputs with respect to the ones explicitly requested by the user;
4. connects properly to the other entities requested by the user through DD relationships.

Information from the Knowledge Base Proxy can be valuable in the entity extraction phase; query terms can be associated with specific entities or attributes by looking at KBP indexes; in particular, terms such as "Times square" or "Central Park" help situating the query's location within New York, and terms such as "Angelina Jolie" or "Brad Pitt" are mapped to actor's names.

KBP relationships can also be very useful in AP selection; a notable case is the use of inheritance associated with IS-A relationships. Assume that one of the query foci is entity E_1 and that we cannot find a suitable AP of E_1 for translating the query, but then assume that entities E_1 and E_2 are linked by an IS-A relationship; then, we may also consider those of E_2 as suitable APs for the query. For example, considering that the IS-A relationship holds in YAGO between *Hostel* and *Hotel*, if we recognize hostel instances such as ("inn", "ymca") in the query, then we may consider using an AP focused on the *Hotel* entity.

Generally speaking, the eligibility of an AP may be formalized as a function giving different weights to the mappings from AP parameters to query terms; for instance, mappings using DD concepts are preferable to mapping using KBP concepts, while use of semantic relationships such as IS-A are weighted by introducing suitable semantic distances, e.g. to a common subsumer node (Jiang and Conrath, 1997).

4.3 Step 3: Service Interface Selection

After APs are selected, each AP should be associated with exactly one service interface. Since by construction service interface parameters and AP parameters match directly, selection at this level is based on additional context knowledge, that can be inferred from the query, for instance by looking for the best implementation that covers the instances used in the query. This can be obtained by exploiting the defined selectors and the Knowledge Base Proxy; for instance, suppose that the user is looking for movies in San Francisco. If the available SIs cover Canada, the US, and the West Coast respectively, one can exclude the first one and prefer the third one over the second one. We next exemplify natural language question processing within a QA use case.

5 A Question Answering Scenario

Let us assume that our Semantic Annotation Framework consists of the Domain Diagram in Figure 1 and YAGO as a reference knowledge base. We suppose that the natural language query q = "Where is a theatre that shows an action movie near Times Square?" is issued by via a search engine-style interface. To understand q, we first need to process it to extract relevant domain information, i.e. its entities and attributes; then, a logical query must be formulated to represent the semantics of q in terms of service marts, APs and service interfaces.

The entity/attribute extraction phase makes high usage of the KBP, which in turns contains YAGO resources supporting the identification of landmarks such as "Times Square", and the instance index in each KBP attribute which allows to directly match a natural language string with the instance of a specific DD entity attribute (e.g. "Times Square" as a possible value for the DD attribute *CurrentPosition.address*). Similar analysis may be used to recognize "action" as a value for the *genre* attribute of entity *Movie*. As a result, we are able to annotate q with DD attribute values, having:
q_{ann} = "Where is a theater that shows an *Movie.genre*[action] movie near *CurrentPosition.address*[Times Square]?"

Syntactic analysis conducted via the Stanford parser (Klein and Manning, 2003) will return the tree in Figure 5, which we name q_{tree}.

Note that q_{tree} contains a main clause ($main$) "Where is a theater" with a clearly distinguishable sub-clause (sub) "that shows an action movie near Times Square", introduced by **SBAR**.

Now, a focus extraction approach such as e.g. the one in (Li et al., 2009) allows us to extract the syntactic focus of both $main$ and sub, i.e. "theatre" resp. "movie"; in particular, $main$, whose focus is "theatre", is mapped to the **Theater** service mart thanks to a simple lookup of the KBP that shows that the two words are synonyms (*Theater* is the preferred meaning of the string "theatre" in YAGO).

Next, a suitable AP is identified for each focus entity. Let us assume that the only available AP for **Movie** is

AP1 `GET Movie BY Movie.genre`

returning movies based on their genre, and that the available APs for **Theater** are

AP2 `GET Theater WITH Movie BY CurrentPosition`

AP3 `GET Theater WITH Movie BY Movie.title`

respectively returning theaters based on the current position and based on the titles of movies they show. The annotation of q suggests AP2 as the most eligible AP. In turn, sub, whose focus is "movie", may be directly mapped to the **Movie** service mart; we then select AP1, its only AP.

Finally, joining AP1 and AP2 to fully express the semantics of q and get to a logical query (e.g. the SeCoQL query in Figure 4) requires a number of additional actions.

First, the values of *Movie.title*, appearing as AP2's output and AP1's input, must match (`ON` predicated of the `JOIN` clause in Figure 4). Secondly, the KB can be used to obtain the mapping of "Times Square" to "New York City"; this in turn allows to identify the theater's country via KB. The latter piece of information is used both to infer a query parameter (`WHERE $W='US'` in Figure 4) and to select a service interface for **Theater** associated with US theaters (`USING S2` in Figure 4).

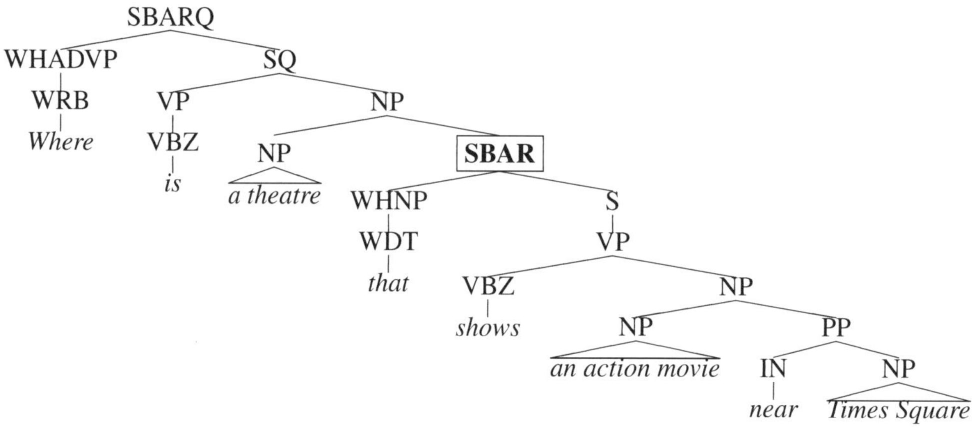

Figure 3: Top syntactic parse tree of the question "Where is a theatre that shows an action movie near Times Square?" according to the Stanford Parser (Klein and Manning, 2003). A subordinate clause is introduced by **SBAR**

```
DEFINE QUERY Cinema($X:String,
             $U:String, $V:String) AS
SELECT M.*, T.* FROM
    AP1(Movie.genre: $X) AS M USING S1
  JOIN
    AP2(Theater.addr: $U, Theater.city: $V,
    Theater.country: $W) AS T USING S2
  ON M.Movie.title=T.Movie.title
WHERE $W='US'
```

Figure 4: SQL-like query representing "Where is a theatre that shows an action movie near Times Square?". `S1` and `S2` denote service interfaces implementing `AP1` and `AP2`, respectively.

6 Conclusions

This paper discusses issues and opportunities offered by Question Answering over data services, which may be regarded as a natural next step of IR with respect to QA over unstructured documents (a consolidated discipline) and over semantic resources (a relatively recent one).

The main issues of QA over data services involve on the one hand the mapping from natural language questions to a semantic representation of the domain and functionalities covered by such services, and on the other the acquisition of the necessary parameters in order to execute physical queries over the latter.

As a possible solution toward this goal, this paper illustrates an architecture that registers service interfaces within an ER domain model where entities, relationships and attributes are sourced from an open-domain universal knowledge base (i.e. YAGO). This approach is motivated by the argument that aligning the semantics of data services with the semantics of natural language queries is the first step towards Question Answering over Web services.

However, the challenge of QA over data services is far from being reached. Future work in this direction chiefly involves 1) efficient strategies (e.g. dialog-based) to acquire service interface parameters from the user in order to feed them to a query execution engine, and 2) effective answer extraction and presentation approaches.

Acknowledgments

Part of the research reported in this paper is in collaboration with Stefano Ceri and Marco Brambilla within the Search Computing project (European Commission IDEAS grant no. 227793).

References

A. Bozzon, D. Braga, M. Brambilla, S. Ceri, F. Corcoglioniti, P. Fraternali, and S. Vadacca. 2011a. Search computing: Multi-domain search on ranked data. In *Proceedings of SIGMOD*.

A. Bozzon, M. Brambilla, E. della Valle, P. Fraternali, and C. Pasini, 2011b. *Integrated Exploration of Linked Data and Semi-structured Web Information*, volume 6585 of *LNCS*. Springer.

D. Braga, M. Grossniklaus, F. Corcoglioniti, and S. Vadacca, 2011. *Efficient Computation of Search Computing Queries*, volume 6585 of *LNCS*, pages 141–155. Springer.

A. Carenini, D. Cerizza, M. Comerio, E. Della Valle, F. De Paoli, A. Maurino, M. Palmonari, and A. Turati. 2008. Glue2: A web service discovery engine with non-functional properties. *Web Services, European Conference on*, 0:21–30.

D. Damljanovic and K. Bontcheva. 2009. Towards enhanced usability of natural language interfaces to knowledge bases. In V. Devedic and D. Gaevic, editors, *Web 2.0 & Semantic Web*, volume 6 of *Annals of Information Systems*, pages 105–133. Springer US.

D. Damljanovic, M. Agatonovic, and H. Cunningham. 2010a. Identification of the question focus: Combining syntactic analysis and ontology-based lookup through the user interaction. In *LREC*.

D. Damljanovic, M. Agatonovic, and H. Cunningham. 2010b. Natural language interfaces to ontologies: Combining syntactic analysis and ontology-based lookup through the user interaction. In *Proceedings of ESWC*, pages 106–120.

E. Delpech and P. Saint-Dizier. 2008. Investigating the structure of procedural texts for answering how-to questions. *LREC2008, Marrakech.*

B. Fazzinga and T. Lukasiewicz. 2010. Semantic search on the web. *Semantic Web Journal.*

D. Fensel, F.M. Facca, E. Simperl, and I. Toma. 2011. *Semantic Web Services*. Springer.

J. Jiang and D. Conrath. 1997. Semantic similarity based on corpus statistics and lexical taxonomy. In *Proceedings of International Conference Research on Computational Linguistics (ROCLING X)*.

E. Kaufmann and A. Bernstein. 2007. How useful are natural language interfaces to the semantic web for casual end-users? In *The Semantic Web*, volume 4825 of *Lecture Notes in Computer Science*, pages 281–294. Springer Berlin / Heidelberg.

E. Kaufmann, A. Bernstein, and R. Zumstein. 2006. Querix: A natural language interface to query ontologies based on clarification dialogs. In *5th International Semantic Web Conference (ISWC 2006)*, pages 980–981. Citeseer.

D. Klein and C.D. Manning. 2003. Accurate unlexicalized parsing. In *Proceedings of the 41st Annual Meeting on Association for Computational Linguistics-Volume 1*, pages 423–430. Association for Computational Linguistics.

C. T. Kwok, O. Etzioni, and D. S. Weld. 2001. Scaling question answering to the web. In *Proceedings of WWW*.

X. Li and D. Roth. 2002. Learning question classifiers. In *Proceedings of ACL*, pages 1–7. Association for Computational Linguistics.

X. Li, Y.Y. Wang, and A. Acero. 2009. Extracting structured information from user queries with semi-supervised conditional random fields. In *Proceedings of SIGIR*, pages 572–579. ACM.

J. Lim and K. Lee. 2010. Constructing composite web services from natural language requests. *Web Semantics: Science, Services and Agents on the World Wide Web*, 8(1):1 – 13.

I. Manolescu, M. Brambilla, S. Ceri, S. Comai, and P. Fraternali. 2005. Model-driven design and deployment of service-enabled web applications. *ACM Trans. Internet Technol.*, 5:439–479, August.

D. Martin, M. Burstein, D. McDermott, S. McIlraith, M. Paolucci, Katia S., D. McGuinness, E. Sirin, and N. Srinivasan. 2007. Bringing semantics to web services with owl-s. *World Wide Web J.*, 10:243–277.

D. L. McGuinness. 2004. Question answering on the semantic web. *IEEE Intelligent Systems*, 19:82–85.

A. Moschitti and S. Quarteroni. 2010. Linguistic kernels for answer re-ranking in question answering systems. *Information Processing & Management*, In Press, Corrected Proof:–.

F. M. Suchanek, G. Kasneci, and G. Weikum. 2007. Yago: a core of semantic knowledge. In *Proceedings of the 16th international conference on World Wide Web*, pages 697–706. ACM.

D. L. Waltz. 1978. An english language question answering system for a large relational database. *Communications of the ACM*, 21(7).

C. Wang, M. Xiong, Q. Zhou, and Y. Yu. 2007. Panto: A portable natural language interface to ontologies. In E. Franconi, M. Kifer, and W. May, editors, *The Semantic Web: Research and Applications*, volume 4519 of *Lecture Notes in Computer Science*, pages 473–487. Springer Berlin / Heidelberg.

An Analysis of Questions in a Q&A Site Resubmitted Based on Indications of Unclear Points of Original Questions

Masahiro Kojima and **Yasuhiko Watanabe** and **Yoshihiro Okada**
Ryukoku University, Seta, Otsu, Shiga, 520-2194, Japan
t10m101@mail.ryukoku.ac.jp, {watanabe, okada}@rins.ryukoku.ac.jp

Topics language processing, pragmatic dimensions

Abstract

In this study, we analyzed how answerers indicated unclear points in questions, and how questioners modified and resubmitted their questions based on indications of unclear points.

1 Introduction

In these days, many of us use question and answer (Q&A) sites where we share our problems and get solutions of them. For example, about 3.11 million questions were submitted to Yahoo! chiebukuro [1] from April/2004 to October/2005. Because of this large numbers of questions, questioners had better submit questions which give enough information to answerers. However, it is difficult to make good questions. For example, in Yahoo! chiebukuro, we often found unclear questions (e.g. Q1 in Figure 1) and their answers where answerers indicated unclear points of the questions (e.g. A1 in Figure 1).

(Q 1) I cannot access a web page which I could read yesterday. What should I do?

(A 1) Show URL.

In (A 1), the answerer pointed out that the questioner did not describe important information to answer the question: URL. Unclear questions may decrease chances of getting good answers. As a result, it is important to investigate supporting methods of making clear questions. One idea is to indicate unclear points of questions, as the questioner of (A 1) did. In order to obtain helpful knowledge and develop a help system for making clear questions, it is important to analyze

- how answerers indicated unclear points in questions, and

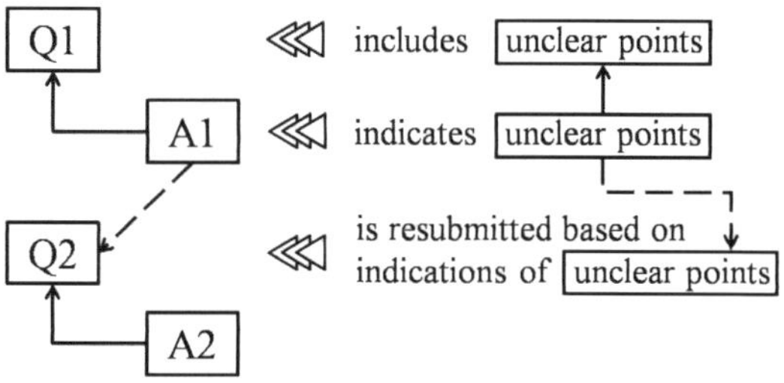

Figure 1: An example of a resubmitted question based on the indication of unclear points in the original question.

- how questioners modified and resubmitted their questions based on indications of unclear points in their original questions.

Our approach differs from previous analyses on Yahoo! Answers (Su et al., 2007) (Adamic et al., 2008). In this study, we used the data of Yahoo! chiebukuro for observation and examination. The data of Yahoo! chiebukuro was published by Yahoo! JAPAN via National Institute of Informatics in 2007 [2]. This data consists of about 3.11 million questions and 13.47 million answers which were posted on Yahoo! chiebukuro from April/2004 to October/2005.

2 Types of indication of unclear points in questions and modification of questions

2.1 Types of indication of unclear points in questions

We observed answers submitted to PC category of Yahoo! chiebukuro and found the following five types of indication of unclear points in questions (Table 1).

TYPE (A1-1) Answerers wanted detailed accounts of what questioners did.

(Q 2) I got a warning from Symantec. How do I extend the software license.

[1] Yahoo Answers in Japan. http://chiebukuro.yahoo.co.jp

[2] http://research.nii.ac.jp/tdc/chiebukuro.html

Table 1: Types of indication of unclear points in questions

TYPE	indication of unclear points in questions
A1-1	detailed accounts of what questioners did
A1-2	detailed accounts of what happened
A1-3	detailed accounts of conditions
A1-4	information other than (A1-1), (A1-2), and (A1-3)
A1-5	unhelpful solution

(A 2) Did you buy an extension key?

TYPE (A1-2) Answerers wanted detailed accounts of what happened.

(Q 3) When I try to maximize my IE window, it is positioned about 2cm below from the top of the screen! What should I do?

(A 3) What's there? blank?

TYPE (A1-3) Answerers wanted detailed accounts of conditions. For example, the indication of (A 1) is classified into this type.

TYPE (A1-4) Answerers wanted detailed accounts of information which were not asked in answers of TYPE (A1-1), (A1-2), and (A1-3).

(Q 4) I don't know the connection type. What should I do?

(A 4) Which connection type do you want to know?

TYPE (A1-5) Answerers submitted solutions, however, they were not helpful to solve questioners' problems. In these cases, answerers did not indicate unclear points of questions. However, we think these unhelpful solutions are one type of indication of unclear points of questions. This is because these unhelpful solutions often made questioners aware of unclear points of their questions. For example, the answerer of (A 5) showed one solution with detailed instruction. The questioner of (Q 5) tried to solve his/her problem according to the instruction and found the solution was unhelpful.

(Q 5) Windows XP crashed. How do I boot my computer?

(A 5) Just put a recovery disc into CD/DVD drive. And restart your PC.

(Q 6) Windows XP crashed. I put a recovery disc into CD drive, but my PC didn't work. How do I boot my computer?

Table 2: Types of modification of questions based on indication of unclear points

TYPE	modification of questions
Q2-1	added explanation based on the indication
Q2-2	added explanation based on other information
Q2-3	described the solution was unhelpful
Q2-4	asked about unknowns in the indication
Q2-5	resubmitted in disregard of the indication

2.2 Types of modification of questions

We observed resubmitted questions in PC category of Yahoo! chiebukuro and found the following five types of modification of questions (Table 2).

TYPE (Q2-1) Questioners added explanations based on the indications of unclear points to their questions and resubmitted them. In this type, it is likely that answerers asked about what questioners knew or could find out easily.

(Q 7) How do I reset my iMac to default settings, except IE and Outlook settings.

(A 7) Show the versions of OS, IE, and Outlook Express.

(Q 8) How do I reset my iMac to default settings, except IE and Outlook settings. My mac OS is version 9 and both IE and Outlook are version 5.

TYPE (Q2-2) Questioners added explanations based on information other than the indications to their questions and resubmitted them. In this type, it is also likely that answerers asked about what questioners knew or could find out easily.

(Q 9) Can I boot my XP PC with Windows 98 HDD?

(A 9) Did you install 98 first? You cannot boot your PC by using Windows 98 if your primary OS is XP.

(Q 10) Can I boot my XP PC with Windows 98 HDD? I don't want to set up a dual boot system. I want to know my PC gets in trouble when I boot it with Win 98 HDD.

TYPE (Q2-3) In resubmitted questions, questioners described that solutions received from answerers were unhelpful to solve their questions. For example, in (Q 6), the questioner described the solution received from the answerer of (A 5) was unhelpful to solve his/her problem. In this type, it is likely that answerers showed one solution which questioners did not know.

TYPE (Q2-4) In resubmitted questions, questioners asked about unknown points in the indication received from answerers. For example, the questioner of (Q 11) received one solution and got the key to solve his/her problem: module deletion. However, he/she did not know it and submitted (Q 12) for requesting detailed information about it.

(Q 11) I removed all macros from my excel file. Then, whenever I open the file, excel asks me if I want to enable/disable macros. How do I stop it?

(A 11) Open visual basic editor and delete the module.

(Q 12) I removed all macros from my excel file. Then, whenever I open the file, excel asks me if I want to enable/disable macros. I want to stop it. The module should be deleted by using visual basic editor. But, how do I do it?

TYPE (Q2-5) Questioners resubmitted almost the same questions as they had. They did not mentioned any kinds of information received from answerers. For example, in (Q 14), the questioner did not mention any kinds of information described in (A 14) although he/she selected (A 14) as a best answer.

(Q 13) My optical mouse is faulty. The cursor sometimes freezes. Is it end of life?

(A 13) Look the back side and remove dust gathered around the red light.

(Q 14) My optical mouse is faulty. The cursor sometimes freezes. Is it end of life?

3 Extraction of original and resubmitted questions and their answers from Yahoo! chiebukuro

We intended to extract

- original questions which included unclear points (e.g. Q1 in Figure 1),
- answers which indicated unclear points in the original questions (e.g. A1 in Figure 1),
- resubmitted questions based on the indications of unclear points in the original questions (e.g. Q2 in Figure 1), and
- answers to the resubmitted questions

from PC category of Yahoo! chiebukuro in the next way.

step 1 extract an answer which indicated unclear points in a question (e.g. A1 in Figure 1). This kind of answer can be extracted by using a method based on machine learning techniques (Isogai et al., 2009).

step 2 extract the question which had the answer extracted in step 1 (e.g. Q1 in Figure 1). This question is regarded as an original question.

step 3 extract the first question submitted by the questioner after he/she received the answer extracted in step 1.

step 4 examine whether the questions extracted in step 1 and step 3 met one of the following conditions:

- they shared more than 10 content words when both of them consisted of more than 20 content words, or
- they shared more than 5 content words.

When one of the conditions was satisfied, the question extracted in step 3 is regarded as a resubmitted question (e.g. Q2 in Figure 1).

step 5 extract the answers to the resubmitted question extracted in step 4 (e.g. A2 in Figure 1).

4 Experimental results

We applied our method described in section 3 to 171848 questions and 474687 answers which were submitted to PC category of Yahoo! chiebukuro from April/2004 to October/2005, and extracted 4271 cases of questions and their answers. Among them, we selected 200 cases randomly and found 133 cases of them where

- an original question (e.g. Q1 in Figure 1),
- the answer which indicated unclear points in the original questions (e.g. A1 in Figure 1),
- the resubmitted questions based on the indication of unclear points in the original questions (e.g. Q2 in Figure 1), and
- the answers to the resubmitted questions (e.g. A2 in Figure 1)

were extracted adequately. We observed these 133 cases and show

Table 3: The results of the analyses: (1) how answerers indicated unclear points in original questions (A1-1, 2, 3, 4, and 5), (2) how questioners utilized indications in answers when they resubmitted their questions (Q2-1, 2, 3, 4, and 5). The numbers in parentheses are the numbers of best answers.

(a) 122 cases where questioners obtained good answers.

	A1-1	A1-2	A1-3	A1-4	A1-5	total
Q2-1	5 (5)	15 (14)	21 (16)	4 (4)	10 (10)	55 (49)
Q2-2	0 (0)	1 (1)	1 (1)	7 (6)	6 (4)	15 (12)
Q2-3	1 (1)	0 (0)	0 (0)	0 (0)	18 (14)	19 (15)
Q2-4	1 (1)	4 (3)	0 (0)	0 (0)	12 (10)	17 (14)
Q2-5	0 (0)	4 (4)	1 (1)	1 (1)	10 (8)	16 (14)
total	7 (7)	24 (22)	23 (18)	12 (11)	56 (46)	122 (104)

(b) 11 cases where questioners did not obtain good answers.

	A1-1	A1-2	A1-3	A1-4	A1-5	total
Q2-1	0 (0)	0 (0)	0 (0)	0 (0)	0 (0)	0 (0)
Q2-2	0 (0)	0 (0)	0 (0)	1 (1)	0 (0)	1 (1)
Q2-3	0 (0)	0 (0)	0 (0)	0 (0)	0 (0)	0 (0)
Q2-4	0 (0)	0 (0)	0 (0)	0 (0)	0 (0)	0 (0)
Q2-5	0 (0)	2 (1)	2 (1)	1 (1)	5 (4)	10 (7)
total	0 (0)	2 (1)	2 (1)	2 (2)	5 (4)	11 (8)

1. whether questioners obtained good solutions or useful clues by resubmitting their questions, especially, when they added explanations based on indications to their questions.
2. how answerers indicated unclear points in questions.
3. whether questioners gave good evaluations to answerers who indicated unclear points of their questions.
4. how questioners utilized indications of unclear points of their original questions when they resubmitted their questions.

Table 3 shows the results of these analyses.

First, we examined whether questioners obtained good solutions or useful clues by resubmitting their questions. As shown in Table 3, there were 26 cases where questioners resubmitted TYPE (Q2-5) questions (questions resubmitted in disregard of indications), and then, 16 of these 26 cases where questioners obtained good solutions or useful clues. On the other hand, there were 107 cases where questioners resubmitted TYPE (Q2-1), (Q2-2), (Q2-3), and (Q2-4) questions, in other words, they accepted indications from answerers and modified their questions. Then, there were 106 of these 107 cases where questioners obtained good solutions or useful clues. As a result, questioners can increase their chances to obtain good solutions or useful clues when they accepted indications from answerers and modified their questions.

Secondly, we examined how answerers indicated unclear points in questions. As shown in Table 3, TYPE (A1-5) answer (unhelpful solution) was the most common answer. As a result, questioners had chances to recognize unclear points in their questions even if they received unhelpful solutions.

Thirdly, we examined whether questioners gave good evaluations to answerers who indicated unclear points of their questions. As shown in Table 3, there were 112 cases (84%) where questioners gave good evaluations to answerers who indicated unclear points of their questions. On the other hand, in PC category of Yahoo! chiebukuro, 474687 answers were submitted and 171848 of them (36%) were received good evaluations. As a result, many questioners gave good evaluations to answerers who indicated unclear points of their questions.

Finally, we examined how questioners utilized indications of unclear points of their original questions when they resubmitted their questions. In this experiment, there were 107 cases where questioners resubmitted TYPE (Q2-1), (Q2-2), (Q2-3), and (Q2-4) questions, in other words, they accepted indications from answerers and modified their questions. Then, there were 17 of these 107 cases where questioners resubmitted TYPE (Q2-4) questions, in other words, they had unknown points in indications received from answerers and needed to ask about what they were. In other 90 cases, questioners resubmitted TYPE (Q2-1), (Q2-2), and (Q2-3) questions, in other words, they knew or could find out easily what answerers indicated. As a result, just to indicate unclear points in questions is useful to make good questions.

References

Su,Q., Pavlov,D., Chow,J., and Baker,W.: Internet-scale collection of human-reviewed data, WWW2007, (2007).

Adamic,L., Zhang,J., Bakshy,E., and Ackerman,M.: Knowledge Sharing and Yahoo Answers: Everyone Knows Something, WWW2008, (2008).

Isogai,N., Nishimura,R., Watanabe,Y., and Okada,Y.: Information Extraction for Supporting a Learner's Efforts to Recognize What the Learner did not Understand, CSEDU 2009, (2009).

Integrating Knowledge Resources and Shallow Language Processing for Question Classification

Maheen Bakhtyar
Department of CSIM,
Asian Institute of Technology, Thailand.
Department of CS&IT,
University of Balochistan, Pakistan.
Maheen.Bakhtyar@ait.asia

Asanee Kawtrakul
Department of Computer Engineering,
Kasetsart University,Thailand.
NECTEC, Pathumthani,
Thailand.
asanee_naist@yahoo.com

Abstract

Typically, Question Classification (QC) is the first phase in Question Answering (QA) systems. This phase is responsible for finding out the type of the expected answer by having the answer space reduced by pruning out the extra information that is not relevant for the answer extraction. This paper focuses on some *Location* based questions and some *Entity* type questions. Almost all the previous QC algorithms evaluated their work by using the classes defined by Li and Roth (2002). The coarse grained classes *Location* and *Entity* both have fine grained class *Other*. In this paper we target and present the mechanism to create new classes to replace the *Other* classes in *Location* and *Entity* class. Additionally, we also present an automatic hierarchy creation method to add new class nodes using the knowledge resources and shallow language processing. We also show how language processing and knowledge resources are important in the question processing and its advantage on Answer Extraction phase.

1 Introduction

Usually people are interested in the exact answer and do not desire to look for the answer themselves in long list of documents. Exact answer is more interesting and useful than getting a list of documents.

Query analysis, processing or classification phase have been always emphasized. The following examples [1] show the importance of this phase with respect to the Answer Extraction.

Example 1: Who was the first American to walk in space?. The answer sentence obtained is *"In 1965 astronaut Edward White became the first American to "walk" in space during the flight of Gemini 4"*[2]. Suppose the question is classified as *Human:Individual* by some classification mechanism. We notice that the answer line contains the matching string "first American to walk in space" therefore, the answer to the question is to be selected from the remaining part "1965", "Edward White" or "Gemini 4". Correct classification now leads us to the answer *Edward White*.

Example 2: What day and month did John Lennon die?. If this question is classified as *Number:Date*, it means that only date type will be targeted from the text. This implies that the question when correctly classified will give a hint about the answer which helps the system in judging and extracting the answer from the corpus.

The questions can be categorized mainly in two ways i.e. considering the question word and second the answer type. Ray et al. (2010) categorizes the factoid questions first in the categories such as *"who", "why", "what", "where", "how" and "when"* and classify them based on the two level hierarchy of classes defined by Li and Roth (2002) and shown in Table 1.

2 Problem Statements

Question Classification is important and helpful for extracting the answers. A correct and meaningful classification will lead the system to more efficient and correct answer extraction mechanisms. On the other hand, a wrong or meaningless classification will not improve the answer extraction and might become a cause of inaccurate final results.

[1] Questions and answer sentence taken from TREC-10 Text-REtrieval-Conference-10 (2001)

[2] This line is taken from the document number *DOCNO: AP890527-0145* and contains the answer to this question

Table 1: Coarse and Fine grained classes

Coarse	Fine
ABBR	abbreviation, expansion
DESC	definition, description, manner, reason
ENTY	**animal, body, color, creation, currency, disease/medical, event, food, instrument, language, letter, *other*,plant, product, religion, sport, substance, symbol, technique, term, vehicle, word**
HUM	description, group, individual, title
LOC	**city, country, mountain, *other*, state**
NUM	code, count, date, distance, money, order, other, percent, period, speed, temperature, size, weight

2.1 Insufficient classes in the taxonomy

Question classes defined and labeled in UIUC[3] dataset by Li and Roth (2002) are most widely used in the previous work (Quan et al. (2011), Song et al. (2011), Yu et al. (2010), Buscaldi et al. (2010), Huang et al. (2007) and Boldrini et al. (2009)). Many of the researchers developed their systems using these classes and the labeled question dataset. In the labeled dataset, if a question is not mapped to some class, it is placed into the fine grained class *Other*. Assigning to a class *Other* is not very helpful in the answer extraction. For example, in case of *Location* category, *Location:Other* will only prune out *city, country, mountain* and *state* as possible answer categories. Therefore, a close analysis of questions belonging to this class is needed and a new set of classes is required to overcome this deficiency.

We currently focus on two of the coarse grained classes; *Location* and *Entity*; and all their fine grained classes. It is also observed that many of the fine grained classes are missing in the existing class hierarchy which needs to be mapped to the questions. For instance, the class *river, lake* or any other *water body* is not present in the existing class taxonomy whereas some questions require such classes e.g. the question *What body of water are the Canary Islands in ?* is currently placed in class *LOC:Other* by Li and Roth (2002). This assigned class neither gives an exact hint nor helps to filter the candidate answers. Whereas, mapping it to a class such as *waterbody* makes it more meaningful and easier to find the answers. Similarly, the question *"what is Bill Gates of Microsoft e-mail address"* ? is labeled as *LOC:Other* by the authors. If this question is searched using a search engine, a lot of documents will be returned having all the key concepts in the question. A chunk of text containing the answer is as follows, *"All the Good Emails get sent to another Bill Gates Email Address, which he checks twice a week. Because He knows everyone will be looking for his email address under @microsoft.com. The Employees who checks his email under billg@microsoft.com send it to the one he checks"* [4]. This chunk from the document contains all the question keywords. Without the classes defined, we do not know which part of the chunk is more important. Whereas, if we determine that the answer should be an email address, then we only need to target the email addresses in the text without taking care of the rest of the document. Therefore, the detail of classes and subclasses is needed to cover more and more questions instead of assigning them to the *LOC:Other* class.

Li and Roth (2002) show that among 500 questions in TREC 10, 62% of the location questions belong to the class *Other*. The highest number of questions lie under the location category *Other* which is actually not very helpful or meaningful in extracting the answer. It means that about 62% of the location questions will be answered during the answer extraction phase without making use of the classes, despite the efforts put into classification phase. Similarly, 13% of the entity questions belong to the class *Other*. *Entity* class has 22 fine grained classes and the large number of questions are mapped to *Other* after *animal* and *substance*. Later, Li and Roth (2006) again gave a statistics of distribution of questions in each class of TREC 10 and 11 Text-REtrieval-Conference (1999 to 2007) questions, collectively. They observed that out of 1000 questions, 195(19.5%) are *Location* based. In *Location* based questions, there are 22.6% questions mapped to class *city*, 10.8% questions about class *country*, 2.6% about *mountain*, 58.5% are mapped to class *other*, and 5.6% questions are mapped to class *state*.

One of the main advantage of replacing the class *Other* with fine grained classes is that it makes assignment of a single question to multiple classes/-

[3] http://cogcomp.cs.illinois.edu/Data/QA/QC/

[4] http://email.about.com/b/2009/05/30/how-can-i-email-bill-gates-what-is-bill-gatess-email-address.htm

subclasses more efficient and effective. A question may implicitly belong to all the subclasses thus, it increases the class coverage.

2.2 Unavailability of automatic class creation mechanism in the hierarchy

In the previous section we show that the new hierarchy of classes and subclasses is needed and effective for efficient answer extraction. Creating new classes manually for each and every possible question is impossible and we need an automatic mechanism to create and assign new classes. Li and Roth (2002) presented a two level hierarchy with a fixed number of classes. Whereas a more general method to create and assign new classes to the questions is required. The new classes may be organized in any number of levels in the hierarchy and can be assigned accordingly.

Our target is to fill the gap of the unavailable classes. We propose a technique that automatically creates new classes and classify the questions having *"what |which NP ... "* pattern. Our technique is based on the language processing and external knowledge resources.

3 Methodology

In this section we propose a methodology for creating the hierarchical structure that represents the classes, and the mechanism to automatically add new classes into the hierarchy.

3.1 Classes in form of a hierarchy

We propose an algorithm that creates hierarchical class taxonomy by placing the existing classes into appropriate position in the tree, and add new classes which are missing in the previous taxonomy, as shown in Figure 1. The question *"Which is the largest island in Thailand?"* is previously mapped to the class *LOC:Other* because there is not any appropriate class available. The *LOC:Other* class does not help much to extract the answer from the given text chunk *"Phuket is now Thailand's most important tourist destination, offering a variety of beaches, attractions and exciting night life. Koh Phuket is Thailand's largest Island. It is 50 km long north to south and 21 km wide and joined to the mainland by Sarasin bridge.Phuket has been inhabited since the early days of mankind by ancient tribes and this still keeps archaeologists occupied to find out the history from the early days.*[5]*"*. If the same question is mapped to the class *LOC:PHY:Natural:Island* or even if to the class *LOC:PHY:Natural*, it will help to locate the *natural locations* or *islands* inside Thailand from the given text chunk.

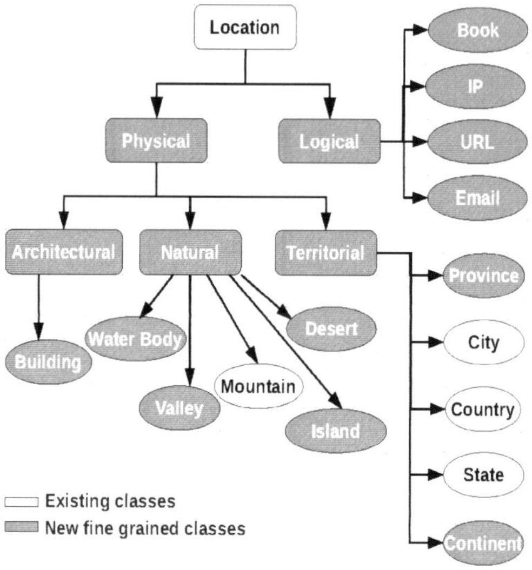

Figure 1: Location Class Hierarchy

Similarly, the question mentioned in the previous section, *"What is Bill Gates of Microsoft e-mail address"* ?, if mapped to subclass *LOC:Logi:Email* or to class *LOC:Logi* will give the hint that some logical location such as URL, email (note that they have fixed patterns and can be extracted easily from the text chunk) is required as an answer. The two classes *Physical* and *Logical* are created by hand and later the subclasses can be inserted.

3.2 Automatic class creation in the hierarchy

In this problem, we will target the questions having the pattern *"what |which NP ... "*. The questions starting with the *What* and *Which* question words, followed by a Noun Phrase (NP), have their expected answer type inside the NP. The expected answer type/question class will be the focus of the NP.

We examined the distribution of the target pattern questions over the existing class hierarchy. We used 1500 questions consisting of 1000 training questions available at UIUC, and 500 questions from TREC 10. We observed that 23% of the questions belong to class *Entity* and 16% belong to class *Location*. Out of these, 16% and 54% belong to classes *ENTY:Other* and *LOC:Other* re-

[5]http://www.beachpatong.com/

spectively. We also observed that 30% of the *ENTY:Other* and 54% of the *LOC:Other* questions are of our target pattern *"what |which NP ... "*. It shows that the proportion of question matching this pattern seems adequate to get started. Therefore, we will focus on the class *Entity:Other* and its subclasses as shown in Figure 2. The similar approach can be applied to the *LOC:Other* class with separate set of patterns e.g. the question *"which part of the university has most trees?"* is a *Location* question having no defined class in the initial hierarchy as well as in the newly created hierarchy shown in Figure 1. Now, the same idea can be applied to this class using different set of patterns, but to keep the initial work simple, we target the subset of question classes and question patterns. Once we have developed a system to add new nodes for this set of questions, we can define similar algorithms for the other set of questions.

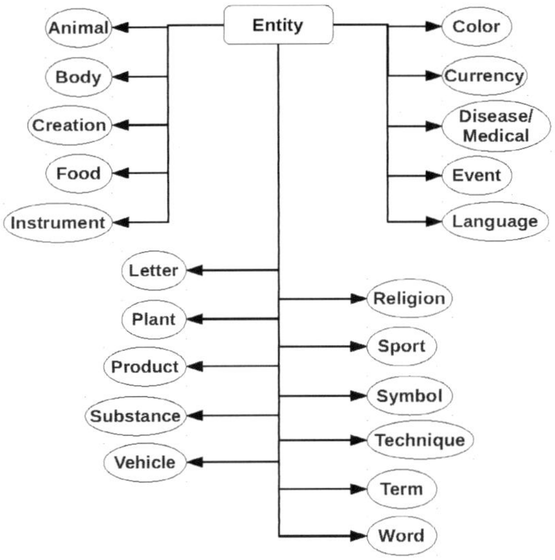

Figure 2: Entity Class Hierarchy

3.2.1 Noun Phrase and Head Noun

Noun phrases have a head noun surrounded by some modifiers such as possessives, adjectives. For example, *"Which **Thailand's island** has highest number of tourists?"* or *"Which **dark green plant** is beneficial to fight cancer? "*

After the first NP is identified in the question, the next task is to determine the head noun e.g. *island* and *plant* in the examples above. Head noun is the target focus of the question and also a candidate class to be added as a node in the hierarchy. For example, in the question *what four forms does gold occur in?* has NP *four forms* and the head noun in this NP is the *forms* which is a candidate new node in the hierarchy. Similarly, the question *"which fungi cause the skin infection?"* has NP and head noun *fungi* and is a candidate for the class in the classes hierarchy.

3.2.2 Adding a class based on similarity calculation and knowledge resources

After finding the focus of the NP i.e. the candidate class for the hierarchy, we cannot directly add the node in the hierarchy. Adding each and every candidate class directly into the hierarchy will make the hierarchy grow very rapidly. We need to consider the relationship between the candidate class and the existing classes before adding a new node. Therefore, first we calculate the similarity between the new candidate and the existing nodes in the hierarchy. If the similarity value between candidate class and some existing class is greater than a threshold t then that existing class is assigned to the candidate class, otherwise a new node is added. The basic framework is shown in Figure 3.

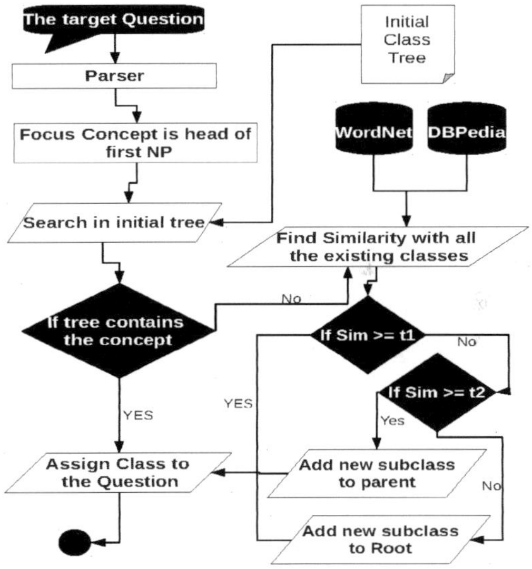

Figure 3: Entity Classification Framework

For calculating the similarity, we use two knowledge resources; WordNet Miller (1995) and DBPedia[6]. DBPedia is the structured version of Wikipedia and one of the largest structured data available online. We use two knowledge bases to cross check and support the answers from both the resources. After calculating the similarity based on WordNet and DBPedia, an average similarity value is used to compare with the threshold val-

[6]http://wiki.dbpedia.org/

ues. We take two threshold values t_1 to classify the question using existing classes and t_2 to add new node as a sub-class of some existing class, where $t_1 > t_2$. If the similarity value is less than both the threshold values then the new node is created but as a child of the root node. The basic algorithm is shown in Algorithm 1. In the algorithm, *AssignClass(Q, some_class)* classifies the question Q as *some_class*. *InsertChildToParent(some_child,some_parent)* creates the class *some_child* as a child of class *some_parent*.

Algorithm 1 Classification

```
Require: A natural language question Q
Require: Threshold values t1 and t2
  NP := First Noun Phrase after the Question Word
  candidate := Extracted Head Noun from NP
  root := Root of the tree
  n := Number of tree nodes
  for i = 1 to n do
    SimWN :=Sim_OSS(node[i], candidate) using WordNet
    SimDB :=Sim_OSS(node[i], candidate) using DBPedia
    similarity := (SimWN + SimDB )/2
    if similarity≥ t1 then
      AssignClass(Q,node[i])
      BREAK LOOP
    end if
    if similarity≥ t2 then
      InsertChildToParent(candidate,[node[i])
      AssignClass(Q,candidate)
      BREAK LOOP
    end if
    InsertChildToParent(candidate, root)
    AssignClass(Q,candidate)
    BREAK LOOP
  end for
```

To find the similarity, we use the algorithm OSS by Schickel-Zuber and Faltings (2007), they reported that their results are better than the existing algorithms. They provide a mechanism to find the semantic relatedness of two concepts.

A high value of Similarity function (Sim_{OSS}) means the concepts are highly related. This value depends on the distance between one concept to another in the Ontology; WordNet and DBPedia in our case.

There is a relationship between the similarity value and the size of the hierarchy. If similarity of concepts is low, it compels to add new nodes into the tree. This means the size of the tree will depend on the threshold set for the addition of new nodes. If the threshold value is big, then tree size will increase because most of the new candidate classes will be added as new node. Therefore, a reasonable values of t_1 and t_2 are to be determined for a reasonable number of nodes in the tree. We have set the threshold values manually in our framework, $t_1 = 0.7$ and $t_2 = 0.5$. If the similarity of candidate class with any of the existing classes is greater than t_1, then the question is mapped to that existing class and no new node is added in the tree.

As we know that in the question *"which fungi cause the skin infection?"*, the head noun is *Fungi*. Now, to decide whether this node should be added or not, we find the similarity with the nodes in the existing hierarchy. Similarity calculation for some concepts is shown in Table 2. A high similarity is observed between the concepts *fungus* and *plant*. Therefore, the question will be classified as the type *Plant*.

Table 2: Similarity calculation

	Sim WN	Sim DBP	Avg
Plant-Fungus	0.86	0.7	0.78
Disease-Artery	0.96	0.0	0.48
Disease-Disease	1.0	1.0	1.0
Musical-Event	0.74	0.0	0.37

We used more than one ontologies, as there might be some relationship missing in either of ontologies. Therefore, to cross check the relationship more than one ontologies are used. For example, in case of DBPedia the similarity value is 0 for *Disease-Artery* and *Musical-Event*, whereas WN gives high similarity.

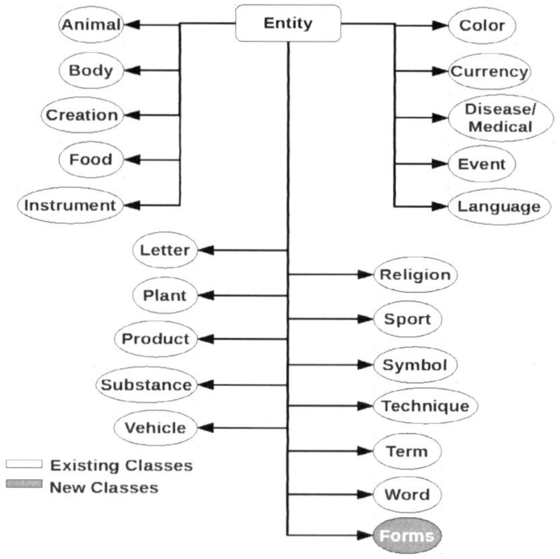

Figure 4: Adding new node

Another question *"what four forms does gold occur in?"* has the target focus (head noun) *forms*. The similarity computed is less than both the threshold values for all the nodes therefore it is added into the hierarchy as a child of the root node.

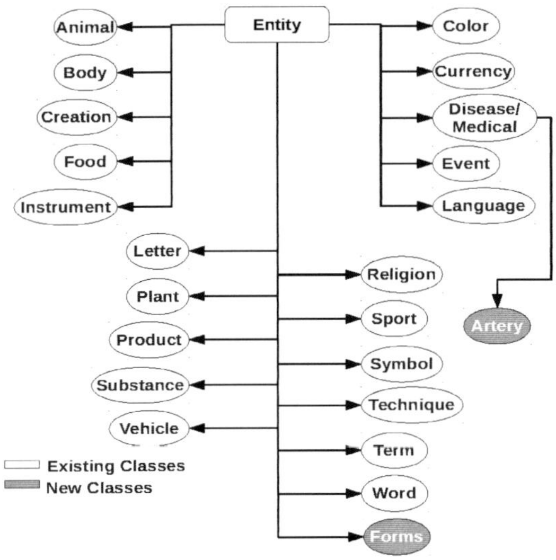

Figure 5: Adding new child

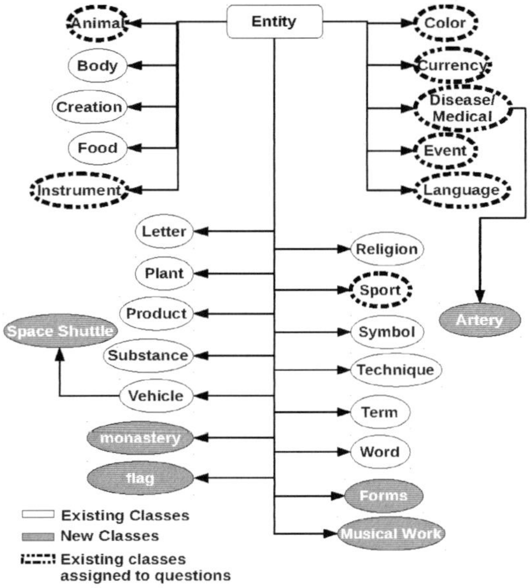

Figure 6: Chunk of new hierarchy

The resulting hierarchy is shown in Figure 4.

For the third case, take the question "what artery is responsible for taking blood from heart to the lungs? ". Assume that after finding similarity between head noun *artery* and all the nodes, none is greater than the threshold t_1. We computed the average similarity of the the head noun with *Disease* as shown in the Table 2. Similarity came out to be $0.48 \approx 0.5$, which is same as t_2, therefore, the new node will be created as a child as shown in Figure 5.

4 Experiments and Discussion

We performed the experiments on set of approximately 20 questions of the pattern *"what |which NP.."* selected from UIUC dataset and some created by hand. To test the system, we first obtain the focus (head noun of NP) of the questions and then check the similarity based on the steps defined in Algorithm 1. Using the rules in the algorithm we populated the hierarchy and assign the classes to the questions. A visual chunk of the resulting tree is shown in Figure 6 and some of the questions are as follows:
Example of questions classified using existing classes are *what gaming devices were dubbed Mississippi marbles and Memphis dominoes?* (mapped to instrument) and *what meter was invented by C.C. Magee in 1935 ?* (mapped to instrument).

We compare the hierarchy built using our approach (Figure 6) with the course and fine grained classes defined by (Li and Roth, 2002) shown in Table 1. We examine some questions and show how the the new classes in the hierarchy can be more helpful to extract the answer.

The question *"What monastery was raided by Vikings in the late eighth century ?"* is currently mapped to *ENTY:Other* whereas using our hierarchy it is mapped to the class *monastery*. If any answer extraction module uses this class instead of *ENTY:Other*, it will skip extra information and will only look for names or information about some monastery. Another example is the question *"which space shuttle was first launced by NASA?"* can be mapped to class *vehicle* which is also informative but our algorithm puts it in the class *Space Shuttle* which makes it more informative. The answer extraction module of any system will now search for the Space Shuttle and its related information.

The initial taxonomy for type *Entity* contained 21 fine grained classes. Our hierarchy, after performing our this initial experiments, had total of 27 classes. It means 22% of the hierarchy consists of new classes. 33% of the newly created classes are added as the sub-classes of some existing class and the remaining are added as direct child of the root.

Our main focus is to develop a more informative class hierarchy. The hierarchy contains more informative fine grained classes which will help the answer extraction phase to locate the answer more precisely. We do not present a complete classification scheme but initially only for the specific pattern of questions as discussed earlier.

Answer extraction phase requires the question to be classified in some manner. If a classification mechanism is developed by using our set of classes, then answer extraction technique be more helpful to extract the answer.

5 Conclusion and Future Work

We propose a new hierarchy for the questions that earlier belonging to the class *Location:Other* or *Entity:Other* . We show that classifying the questions into *"Other"* is not very useful for the answer extraction phase. These two classes are now represented as a hierarchy which is populated using some NLP techniques and knowledge resources i.e. WordNet and DBPedia. We also analyzed how the new hierarchy helped to prune out the extra unnecessary details for efficient answer extraction.

This is the initial work carried out with extremely limited questions. We only focused on the question with a specific pattern for generating the new hierarchy using knowledge resources. We plan to work on the remaining question types and patterns in the future. Moreover, we also plan to target the other coarse classes, "*NUM*" having sub-type "*Other*".
Additionally, we plan to label the questions and publish with the hierarchy obtained for all the questions set so a new set of classes is obtained and is comparable for the other researchers.

References

E. Boldrini, S. Ferrández, R. Izquierdo, D. Tomás, O. Ferrández, and J. L. Vicedo. 2009. A proposal of expected answer type and named entity annotation in a question answering context. In *Proceedings of the 2nd conference on Human System Interactions*, HSI'09, pages 315–319, Piscataway, NJ, USA. IEEE Press.

Davide Buscaldi, Paolo Rosso, José Manuel Gómez-Soriano, and Emilio Sanchis. 2010. Answering questions with an n-gram based passage retrieval engine. *J. Intell. Inf. Syst.*, 34:113–134, April.

Peng Huang, Jiajun Bu, Chun Chen, and Guang Qiu. 2007. An effective feature-weighting model for question classification. In *Proceedings of the 2007 International Conference on Computational Intelligence and Security*, CIS '07, pages 32–36, Washington, DC, USA. IEEE Computer Society.

Xin Li and Dan Roth. 2002. Learning question classifiers. In *Proceedings of the 19th international conference on Computational linguistics*, pages 1–7, Morristown, NJ, USA. Association for Computational Linguistics.

Xin Li and Dan Roth. 2006. Learning question classifiers: the role of semantic information. *Natural Language Engineering*, 12(03):229–249.

George A. Miller. 1995. Wordnet: A lexical database for english. *Communications of the ACM*, 38:39–41.

Xiaojun Quan, Liu Wenyin, and Bite Qiu. 2011. Term weighting schemes for question categorization. *IEEE Trans. Pattern Anal. Mach. Intell.*, 33(5):1009–1021.

Santosh Kumar Ray, Shailendra Singh, and B.P. Joshi. 2010. A semantic approach for question classification using wordnet and wikipedia. *Pattern Recognition Letters*, 31(13):1935 – 1943. Meta-heuristic Intelligence Based Image Processing.

Vincent Schickel-Zuber and Boi Faltings. 2007. Oss: a semantic similarity function based on hierarchical ontologies. In *Proceedings of the 20th international joint conference on Artifical intelligence*, pages 551–556, San Francisco, CA, USA. Morgan Kaufmann Publishers Inc.

Wanpeng Song, Liu Wenyin, Naijie Gu, Xiaojun Quan, and Tianyong Hao. 2011. Automatic categorization of questions for user-interactive question answering. *Inf. Process. Manage.*, 47:147–156, March.

Text-REtrieval-Conference-10. 2001. Trec-10 question answering data.

Text-REtrieval-Conference. 1999 to 2007. Trec qa main page.

Zhengtao Yu, Lei Su, Lina Li, Quan Zhao, Cunli Mao, and Jianyi Guo. 2010. Question classification based on co-training style semi-supervised learning. *Pattern Recogn. Lett.*, 31:1975–1980, October.

A Rule Based Approach for Analysis of Comparative or Evaluative Questions in Tourism Domain

Bidhan Chandra Pal **Pinaki Bhaskar** **Sivaji Bandyopadhyay**
Department of Computer Science and Engineering
Jadavpur University, Kolkata – 700032, India
(bidhan.cstbesus, pinaki.bhaskar)@gmail.com, siva-ji_cse_ju@yahoo.com

Abstract

Comparative or evaluative questions are the non-factoid class of questions that contain comparative or evaluative keywords, which may or may not be directly quantifiable. This entails the need for extraction of comparative and evaluative features, identification of semantic meaning of those features and converting them to quantifiable criteria before data can be obtained from the source text. This paper presents the study of the comparative or evaluative questions along with a rule based approach to syntactically extract and semantically analyze comparative or evaluative features, and give a basic idea to generate the answer.

1 Introduction

Answering of the Comparative or Evaluative questions needs some extra effort mainly because of two reasons. The first reason is the extraction of the Comparative or Evaluative keywords and features (CEF) from the question and syntactically and semantically analyzing them. Secondly, the non-quantifiable Comparative or Evaluative expressions have to be transformed into quantifiable criteria so that appropriate answer can be generated.

The Comparative or Evaluative expressions mainly belong to the adjective (like good, better, best) or the adverbs followed by the adjective (like more popular, most popular). The expression depicts the degree of comparison (e.g. general or positive/ negative, comparative, superlative). The Comparative or Evaluative expression may (for example, cheapest hotel to stay in Las Vegas where 'cheapest' is the comparative expression) or may not be (for example, best hotel to stay in Las Vegas where 'best' is comparative expression) directly quantifiable. So, a mechanism is necessary to convert all the Comparative or Evaluative expressions into quantifiable criteria. The Comparative and Evaluative Features (CEF) include the entity upon which comparison is done (e.g. all hotels in Las Vegas) and the constraints, which are used to choose the most appropriate entity. In brief, the task of question analysis part can be divided into 3 basic operations.

1. Extraction of Comparative or Evaluative Expression and CEFs.
2. Classification of question according to user information need.
3. Transforming the Comparative or Evaluative expression into quantifiable criteria.

Another issue with the comparative or evaluative question is that, it requires great deal of domain knowledge to transform comparative or evaluative keywords into quantifiable criteria. For example, if 'best' is the comparative keyword and used as 'best hotel' (e.g., what are the best hotels in Las Vegas?) in tourism domain and 'best insurance policy' (e.g. what are the best insurance policy for my child education?) in business domain then system has different set of paradigms to transform 'best' into quantifiable criteria. The topic is elaborately discussed in section 3.

In the next section, the related works of the Comparative or Evaluative questions are described. The challenges are described in Section 3. In the next section 4, the degree of comparison is described. The decomposition of non-quantifiable expressions is described in Section 5. Section 6 elaborates our approach to build the question analyzer. System evaluation is described in Section 7. Future works are discussed in Section 8.

2 Related works

Friedman (1989) presents a general approach to process comparative expressions by syntactically treating them to conform to a standard form containing the comparative operator and the clauses that are involved in the comparison. Another approach would be to automatically extract comparative relations in sentences via machine learning.

Olawsky (1989) attempts to study the semantic context by generating a set of candidate interpretations of comparative expressions. Then, the user is prompted to choose among these to specify his intent.

Kennedy (2006) proposed that comparisons may be in relation to properties within the same object, degree of comparisons of the same property between different objects, or different properties of different objects. The properties at stake in the comparison are embedded in the semantics of the words in the question, and possibly in the context that comes with the question. To date, there is obviously no widely available lexical resource containing an exhaustive list of comparative predicates, applied to precise terms, together with the properties involved. These can possibly be derived, to a limited extent, from existing resources like Frame-Net or from ontology where relationships between concepts and terms can be mapped. However, this is tractable for very simple situations, and in most cases, identifying those properties is a major challenge.

Nathalie et al (2009) have proposed the technique to handle comparative and evaluative question answering for business domain. They have proposed the procedure to identify the terms in the question based on which comparison or evaluation can be done.

This paper gives the idea of a question answering system which is capable of handling comparative and evaluative questions related to tourism domain and attempts to resolve the challenges identified by Patrick et al (2009).

3 Challenges

Patrick et al (2009) show the challenges that the comparative and evaluative question answering system face.

Type of comparison: Comparisons may be the relation to properties within the same object, or degree of comparisons of the same property between different objects, or different properties of different objects. In some simple situations, Jindal and Liu (2006) show that comparative relations in sentences can be extracted automatically via machine learning. Their approach determines whether the expression is non-equal gradable, equative, or superlative. In this paper a rule based technique is used to explore in depth semantic and conceptual issues and their dependence to context, users, and domains.

Determining semantic meaning and converting to quantifiable measures: The properties at stake in the comparison are embedded in the semantics of the words in the question, and possibly in the context that comes with the question. To date, there is obviously no widely available lexical resource containing an exhaustive list of comparative predicates, applied to precise terms, together with the properties involved. However, this is tractable for very simple situations, and in most cases, identifying those properties is a major challenge. Various ways to accurately identify these properties through different resources (like Generative Lexicon) in the tourism domain have been explored.

Ambiguity of Comparative Expression: The standard of comparison (i.e., the value) may be different based on the context, i.e., depending on the object that it is associated to and on the type of expression. Properties of expression may be underspecified and/or polysemous and would gain context only when associated with the object. One such predicate is 'best'.

Best Place to go: type of weather of the place, popularity to visit, number of famous tourist spots.

Best Hotel to stay: type of Hotel (1 star, 3 star,5 star), types of rooms (AC, Non AC, Double Bed etc) available, Fare of the room & Other facilities

Best way to reach: Type of communication (Train, Bus, Flight etc), duration of journey, fare of the journey etc.

To automatically determine the properties, including default values, to be used in the evaluation, other available sources indicating some range of values may be tapped, as is done in answer fusion. But rather than retrieving the partial answer, properties needed for evaluation must be retrieved or inferred. Values may be either numerical values (where comparisons are quite easy to handle) or textual values (that are often discrete). It is then necessary to define comparative scales along basic properties so that those values get ordered. This is a major challenge for our work.

Processing superlatives and other forms of quantification related to comparisons: Superlatives and other forms of quantifications in connection with comparative expressions can also be used on top of the basic evaluative expressions. Consider the question:

Which is the best hotel to stay in Delhi?

"Best hotel" entails different dimensions from being conservative. In the context of tourism, evaluation could be in terms of variety of room; rent of the hotel, satisfactory room service, availability of restaurant, bar, summing pool and other facilities. Also sometime it is not explicitly mentioned the boundary of the entity for superlative question (for example hotels). If a strict evaluation of all these criteria is done, the result may not be complete or accurate. So it may be the better approach to rank the result and show top 10 results than showing a single answer.

Domain dependency: Transformation of the comparative expression into quantifiable criteria needs domain knowledge. The comparative expression and associated features contain the semantic meaning of the question. The semantic meaning of the features is changed in different domain. So the same comparative expression can be translated into different quantifiable criteria depending on which domain question is raised. Domain dependency is a biggest problem in analysis of the comparative and evaluative questions.

4 Determine Degree of Comparison and Evaluation

It is observed that the Comparative Expressions may be either adjective (e.g., cheaper, best etc.) or adverb associated with adjective or another adverb (e.g. more/RB popular/JJ, most/RB comfortable/JJ, as/RB fast/RB as/IN, as/RB comfortable/JJ as/IN etc) or quantifiers. In a sentence the comparative expression is placed in adjective chunk preceded by either verb or noun chunk and followed by noun chunk (e.g. *what*/WP (VP (*are*/VBP *the*/DT (NP (*cheapest*/JJS *hotels*/NNS)) *in*/IN (NP (*Las*/NNP *Vegas*/NNP?))))) or (*what*/WP (VP (*are*/VBP (NP (*the*/DT *Las*/NNP *Vegas*/NNP)) (NP (*cheapest*/JJS *hotels*/NNS))))).

The comparative expression can be categorized into three classes according to the nature of comparison.

1. Positive/Negative or General: Positive /Negative or General comparative expression is basically not to compare between entities but to know whether the entity posses the criteria or not.

Example: Is the [Taj Bengal] (entity) [good] (Comparative Expression) [5 star hotel] (criteria)?

2. Comparative: Comparative expressions are those which compare between two entities or two set of entities.

Example: Is [ITC Sonar Bangla] (entity) [better] (Comparative Expression) than [Taj Begal] (entity)? or

Is [ITC Sonar Bangla] (entity) as [good] (Comparative Expression) *as* [*Taj Begal*] (entity)?

3. Superlative: Superlative expressions are those which compare an entity with set of entity based on certain criteria.

Example: Is [Taj Bengal] (entity) [best](Comparative Expression) [5 star hotel in Kolkata] (criteria)?

Sometimes it is seen that the entity is not explicitly defined. For example, the following question does not include the entity information: What are the [best] (Comparative Expression) [5 star hotel in Kolkata] (criteria)?

All relevant entities have to be identified for the above question and then compared according to criteria.

The rules to extract comparative expressions in the present work are discussed in Table 4.

Evaluative expressions: Evaluative expressions are not directly compared but checks whether the criteria are matched or not.

Example: *What are the* [*morning*] (Evaluative Expression) [*flights to Delhi from Kolkata*] (entity)?

It is also important that entity and expression can appear in many places in the sentence. User can also write the previous question in many different ways (like what are the Kolkata to Delhi morning flight? or what are the morning Kolkata to Delhi flight? etc.). So we extract the relevant important information in the form of Comparative and Evaluative Features (CEF).

5 Decompose Non-quantifiable criteria to quantifiable criteria

The comparative or evaluative expressions may not be directly quantifiable. It is the task of the question analyzer to decompose these non-quantifiable expressions to equivalent quantifiable criteria. In the earlier example question, the comparative expression "good 5 star hotels" is not a directly quantifiable expression. To solve this, we follow the human interpretation of answering whether the hotel is a good 5 star Hotel or not. For a human, a hotel is a good 5 Star Hotel if it has adequate rooms with good variety (like single bed, double bed, cottage, suit etc.), quality food and other facilities like gym, swimming pool, disco, library, etc. so the comparative expression 'good' depends on the entity (5 star hotel) features or characteristic that are stated below.

1. Adequate Rooms
2. Varity of Rooms
3. Quality of Food Service
4. Availability of Gym
5. Availability of Summing Pool
6. Availability of Bar
7. Availability of Casino
8. Availability of Disco

So the non-quantifiable comparative expression can be evaluated by the linear combination of the weighted entity features. The entity feature values can be computed by the percentage of matching keywords/phrases for string valued features or the deviation from the range for numerical valued features. The weight of each feature represents user preferences.

6 Our Approach

As we have discussed earlier, our prime target is to extract all important properties (comparative or evaluative expression, its degree of comparison, entity and constraints) or features from the user given question. In this section, we describe the basic idea to analyze the comparative and evaluative questions raised in the tourism domain.

6.1 Why tourism domain?

We have used tourism related question because of two reasons.

1. Tourism is very popular domain where user frequently asked various types of question. So it has rich set of comparative or evaluative questions.
2. Tourism domain has large set of criteria for each entity. So comparison can be done appropriately.

Over 200 questions are collected from different tourism website Q&A section. Rules have been developed with 150 questions. These rules are applied on the rest 50 questions. Here are some questions[1]:

Q1: We plan to visit Andhra Pradesh in December. We live in Kolkata, and will start and end our journey at Vizag and have seven days in hand. We are three families with kids and our budget is moderate. Kindly suggest an itinerary, which must include Araku Valley.

Q2: My family is planning a trip to Khashmir in late October. We plan to spend six days there and will visit Srinagar, Gulmarg, and Pahalgam. Can you suggest good hotel in range of Rs 3000-4000?

Q3: My husband, son and I want to visit Stuttgart, Heidelberg, Salzburg and maybe Munich in May 2010. We live in Mumbai. Is it cheaper to fly to Frankfurt first or to Stuttgart?

6.2 Classification of questions according to information need

All the questions related to tourism domain can be classified into 7 classes according to their information need. The categories are stated below:

Itinerary: The questions where user asks for a suggested itinerary or schedule or planning for visiting a place fall into this category.

Accommodation: The questions where user asks for accommodation, i.e., Hotel detail, Cost to stay, etc for a place fall into this category.

How to Reach: The questions regarding how to visit or reach a place along with transportation details like travel by train, flight and cost of transportation fall into this category.

Best Time to Visit: User asks for the best time to visit a place or whether a specific time is best to visit that place or not.

Getting Around: User asks for details of seeing the tourist spot, buy something, eat/drink in a restaurant etc.

Cost Related Information: User asks for estimated cost to visit a place or per head cost to visit a place.

Miscellaneous: If the question does not classify into any of the above categories then it comes under miscellaneous category.

Table 1 shows the result of classifying 200 questions that are collected.

#	Type of Question	Percentage
1	Itinerary	18%
2	Accommodation	22%
3	Reach Destination	19%
4	Best Time To Visit	9%
5	Getting Around	20%
6	Cost Related Information	8%
7	Miscellaneous	4%

Table 1: % of question occurs in different class

[1]Questions are taken from Ask Marco of Outlook Travelers: http://travel.outlookindia.com/article.aspx?264509

Questions are classified into different classes using set of rules. Rules are nothing but matching string. If a string is present then the question is classified into the corresponding class. The rules are stated in Table 2.

#	Type of Question	Rules (Question Consist of following String)
1	Itinerary	itinerary, chalk out a [trip, tour]
2	Accommodation	[H,h]otels?, [a,A]ccommodations?
3	Reach Destination	travels?, transport
4	Best Time To Visit	[good, best, preferable, suitable] [time, season]
5	Getting Around	site screen, place to visit, tourism spot
6	Cost Related Information	cost per [day, week, head, living], per [day, week, head, living] cost
7	Miscellaneous	If any question was not classified in any of the above six classes then it will be classified as Miscellaneous.

Table 2: Rule for classifying questions into different classes.

6.3 Extraction of CEF

The comparative and evaluative features (CEF) are the features which play useful role to evaluate the answer of the question. CEFs are holding the semantic meaning of the phrases like time of visit, duration of visit, Number of people are going and their description like age (old, kids etc), relation (wife, friends, family, parent) etc. For example CEF holds the information of user opted tour places, his/her purpose of visiting those places, his/her family and relative information who will accompany the user, the time when user wants to go, the time span that user wants to spend, the budget of user, and other user specifications. So answers of the question are heavily dependent on the CEFs present in the question.

Sixteen types of CEF are identified. All of these 16 types of features may not occur in a single question. In these 16 types of CEFs, the place features like <Origin Place> and <Destination Place> etc are included. <Destination Place> is always required and must be present in the question. The various CEFs are now described.

Location Related feature: These features contain the place name where user wants to go/travel/stay etc or the place name from where he/she starts his/her journey or where he/she stays (Origin). Sometimes user also mentions the place name where he/she must want to visit.

Location To: Where user wants to go/visit/travel/see.

Extraction Rule: Location named entity words are preceded by preposition “to”, “include”, “at”

Location From: From where user wants to start his/her journey.

Extraction Rule: Location named entity words are preceded by preposition “from”, “in”.

Must Include Locations: Explicitly mentioned place name where user must visit.

Extraction Rule: Location named entity words are preceded by preposition “must”, “include”.

Similar Locations: User wants to visit the place that is similar (historically, geographically etc) with explicitly mentioned place.

Extraction Rule: Location named entity words are preceded by preposition “similar”, “Likely”.

Time Related Information: These features contain the time related phrase like the time when user wants to travel or duration of his/her travel.

Time to Go: When user plans to go/travel/stay on the place.

Extraction Rule: Noun Phrase consists of Month, Season and Day Expressions.

Month={"january","frebruary","march","april","may","june","july","august","september","october","november","december"};

Season={"summer", "rainy", "monsoon", "winter", "autumn"};

Day={"sunday","monday","tuesday","wednusday","thusday","friday","saturday"};

Time Limit: How many days user wants to spend.

Extraction Rule: Noun Phrase consists of Time Expression

TimeExp={"day","days","month","months","week","weeks","nights","nights","fortnight","fortnights","weekends","weekend","week ends", "week end"};

Team Related Information: This type of feature contains the phrases that carry the information of the number of members with whom user wants to share his/her journey and their details.

Team Member: Number of people who will travel with the user

Extraction Rule: Noun Phrase consists of Team Expression

TeamExpression= {"families", "family", "couple", "men", "women", "man", "woman", "friends", "friend", "colleague"};

Team Details: The relation of other member with the user and their details like age, or disease/weakness etc.

Extraction Rule: Noun Phrase consists of Team Details Expression

TeamDetailsExpression = {"family" ,"husband", "wife", "father", "mother", "son", "daughter", "friends", "young", "old", "kids" etc};

Travel Related Information: These features contain useful information like the budget of travel and purpose of travel etc.

Budget: User may specify the expected budget of their journey.

Extraction Rule: Noun Phrase consists of keyword like "moderate", "cheapest", "budget" or "$", "USD", "'", "Rs", "INR", "£", "EUR", "€", "GBP" followed by Number Expression which consists tag "(CD".

Purpose of Travel: User may specify the purpose of his/her journey like tourism, business, honeymoon, study etc.

Extraction Rule: Noun Phrase consists of Visit Type Expression.

Visit Type= {tour, family tour, business, honeymoon, study, job}

Adjective Modifier: Adjective modifier plays an important role to evaluate the answer. Adjective modifiers like cheapest, best, suitable, affordable, comfortable etc. give different directions of evaluating the answer. User uses adjective modifier to specific their choices.

Extraction Rule: Noun Phrase contains Adjective phrases with JJ or JJS tag or ADJP Phrase.

Specific Type Related Information: Some features are dependent on the type of question.

Accommodation Related These features specify the choice of accommodation of the user. Sometime user specifies the special range of accommodation like government guesthouse, holiday home etc.

Hotel Type: User specifies the type of hotel he/she wants to stay.

Extraction Rule: Noun Phrase contains keyword like "Private Hotels", "Government Hotel", and "Guest House", "Hostel" etc

Hotel Specification: User specifies the criteria that should be met by a hotel, like, 3-star, 5-star, resort, etc.

Extraction Rule: Noun Phrase contains keyword like "hotel", "Inn", "Resort", "Darmasala" etc

Transportation: This feature specifies the choice of transportation of the user, like, flight, bus, train.

Transportation Mode: User may specify his/her liking or disliking of transportation mode while traveling.

Extraction Rule: Noun Phrase contains keyword like "train", "bus", "car", "flight", "fly" etc.

Getting Around: This feature specifies the choice or purpose of Getting Around like to see tourist spot or buy or see market place etc.

Extraction Rule:

Getting Around Choice: User may specify his/her choice to do (See tourist spot, or roam famous market place or eat foods in restaurant etc) while staying at the place.

Extraction Rule: Choice= {sight seen, buy, eat}

The CEFs identified in the three questions are now described.

Q1: We plan to visit [Andhra Pradesh]/*LOCATION_TO* in [December]/*TIME_TO_GO*. We live in [Kolkata]/*LOCATION_FROM*, and will start and end our journey at [Vizag]/*LOCATION_FROM* and have [seven days]/*TIME_LIMIT* in hand. We are [[three families]/*TEAM_MEMBER* with kids]/*TEAM_DETAILS* and our [budget is moderate]/*BUDGET*. Kindly suggest an itinerary, which must include [Araku Valley]/*MUST_INCLUDE_LOCATION*.

Q2: My family is planning a trip to [Khashmir]/*LOCATION_TO* in [late October]/*TIME_TO_GO*. We plan to spend [six days]/*TIME_LIMIT* there and will visit [Srinagar]/*LOCATION_TO*, [Gulmarg]/*LOCATION_TO*, and [Pahalgam]/ *LOCATION_TO*. Can you suggest [good hotel]/*ADJECTIVE_MODIFIER* in range of [Rs 3000-4000]/*BUDGET*?

Q3: [My husband, son and I]/*TEAM_DETAILS* want to visit [Stuttgart]/*LOCATION_TO*, [Heidelberg]/*LOCATION_TO*, [Salzburg]/ *LOCATION_TO* and maybe [Munich]/*LOCATION_TO* in [May 2010]/*TIME_TO_GO*. We live in

[Mumbai]/*LOCATION_FROM.* Is it [cheaper]/*ADJECTIVE_MODIFIER* to [fly]/*TRANSPOTATION_MODE* to [Frankfurt]/*LOCATION_TO* first or to [Stuttgart]/*LOCATION_TO*?

6.4 Determining degree of comparison and Entity Selection

The comparative or evaluative expressions, the entities and the constraints are extracted from the CEFs. Comparative or Evaluative Expression belong to Adjective Modifier. Entity and Constraints are different for different class of question. These are shown in Table 3.

#	Type of Question	Entity to be Compared	Constraints to be considered
1	Itinerary	Location To, Location From, Must Include Location, Location Preference,	Time to Go, Time Limit, Budget, Purpose of Visit
2	Accommodation	Hotel Type	Location To, Location From, Must Include Location, Team Details, Budget, Hotel Specification, Purpose of visit
3	Reach Destination	Transportation Mode	Location To, Location From, Time to Go, Team Details, Budget,
4	Time related Info.	Time to Go	Purpose of Visit, Location To, Must Include Location, Location Preference
5	Getting Around	Getting Around Preference	Time to Go, Team Details, Budget, Purpose of Visit
6	Cost Related Info.	Location To, Must Include Location, Location Preference	Budget, Purpose of Visit

Table 3: Entity and Constrains for different class

Now the degree of comparison is determined from the rules describe in table 4.

Table 5 shows the Comparative or Evaluative Expressions, type of comparison, Entities and Constraints of the questions Q1, Q2 & Q3.

#	Type of Comparison	Rules
1	General or Positive or Negative	1. Adjectives form the list {good, suitable, clean, new, appropriate, preferable, dirty, easy, happy, pretty, reasonable, bad, cheap, large, big, small. fast} appeared in noun chunk. 2. ADJP chunk staring with much or many
2	Comparative	1. Adjective with -er extention and appeared in ADJP chunk and followed by preposition than 2. Adjective or phrase inside as-as (like as soon as possible) 3. ADJP chunk staring with more 4. ADJP chunk containing too
3	Superlative	1. Adjective with -est extension appeared in Noun Chunk or ADJP chunk 2. ADJP chunk staring with most

Table 4: Rules to determine degree of comparison

#	Evaluative/ Type of Comparison	Entity	Constraints
Q1	Evaluative	Andra Pradesh, Vizag, Araku Vally,	December, Seven Days, Budget is moderate
Q2	General Expression: 'good hotel'	Srinagar, Pahelgram, Gulmarg, Hotel, Family tour	Family, six days, Late October, Rs 3000-4000
Q3	Comparative Expression: 'cheaper option'	Frankfrut, Stugart, Mumbai, Fly	May 2010, My husband, son & I,

Table 5: Extracted Entity, Comparative or Evaluative Expression & constrains.

6.5 Decomposing non-quantifiable expression into quantifiable criteria

Now we identify the list of comparative expression that are found in our test set and are not directly quantifiable. They are good, suit/suitable, comfortable, perfect, reasonable, appropriate, clean, safe etc. and their comparative and superlative forms.

Decomposition of non-quantifiable expression is done by the scoring of each feature of the entity. The score of the entity features are computed by the percentage of keyword/phrase matching between the keywords present in the entity feature value and the keywords present in the rules for the string valued features (e.g. variety of rooms for hotel entity) or by the standard deviation from the range for numerical valued features (e.g. rent of the room for hotel entity). The rule set are developed for each non-quantifiable expression for each class of question which contains the keyword set for each entity features by human annotator. So the 'good hotel' comparative expression of Q2 can be evaluated by using the following hotel features.

Good Hotel=
1. Adequate Rooms
2. Varity of Rooms
3. Rent of the rooms
4. Other facilities

From Q2, the system has also extracted the other constraints (e.g. Team Details='Family', Time Limits='six days', Time to Go='Late October' & Budget='Rs 3000-4000'). So the rule for determining good hotel is shown below.

Good Hotel =
1. Adequate Rooms available in Late October
2. Availability of Double bed Rooms, Double bed Ac room, family suit, cottage etc.
3. Room Rent between Rs 3000-4000
4. Availability of family restaurant, room service etc.

So the entity features are scored by the percentage of matching keywords between the rule and feature value. The keywords in the rule are changed according to the constraints present in the question. Here we show how the keywords of the 'variety of room' features are changed for the 'good hotel' comparative expression with different constraints:

If team details consist of friends, colleague, etc and if travel limits are more than 7 days in a place then keywords are *dormitory, single bed, non-ac rooms*.

If team details consist businessman or purpose of travel is business and if a travel limit is less than 7 days in same place then keywords are *suit, cottage, villa* etc.

If team details include husband and wife, or newly married couple and the purpose of travel is honeymoon then keywords are *double bed ac/non ac, family suit, villa* etc.

The comparison is done by ordering the final score of each entity. The final score is evaluated by the weighted average of each entity feature score. Weight of entity features is between 0-5, which represents the user preference. For example if user explicitly mentioned his/her budget in numerical figure (e.g. Rs 3000-4000) then the entity features related with budget (e.g. room rent) has weight 5. If user mentioned its budget as moderate the entity features related with budget (e.g. room rent) has weight 3. If user does not explicitly mentioned his/her budget then the entity features related with budget (e.g. room rent) has weight 1.

Sometimes two or more comparative expressions are semantically close like 'good hotel' & 'appropriate hotel' or 'suitable hotel' so same rule can be followed for those expressions.

Quantifiable adjective are those which can quantify directly like cheap, fast, short, large, big small, high, low etc. So, 'cheapest hotel' means low cost hotel. We just sort the hotel rent in ascending order and show the top 5 results.

7 Evaluation

We have developed the rules with 150 distinct questions and tested it over 50 questions. The system is evaluated by the string matching technique between the system generated tagged questions and the corresponding human annotated tagged questions. The precision and recall are calculated by the formula (1) and (2). Table 6 shows the precision and recall of our system.

$$\text{Precision} = \frac{\text{Matched keywords/phrases}}{\text{System Generated tagged Output}} \quad \ldots (1)$$

$$\text{Recall} = \frac{\text{Matched keywords/phrases}}{\text{Human annotated tagged question/ Gold standard tagged question}} \quad \ldots (2)$$

Objective	Precision	Recall
Classification of Questions	86.5%	84.3%
Extraction of CEFs	86.1%	82.5%
Determine degree of comparison	84.3%	81.2%
Entity Recognition	76.2%	74.8%
Constraints Recognition	72.3%	68.4%
Decomposition of Non-quantifiable expression	71.3%	68.1%

Table 6: Precision and Recall of System

8 Conclusion and Future work

System is somewhat biased because all the rules are manually developed and it requires the great understanding of domain knowledge. In future machine learning technique will be used to extract the rules and to extract more comparative and evaluative features from the question. Extraction of more features means extraction of more semantic information's from question. Sometime user gives unusual information that misleads the system and drives to wrong direction. If we extract semantically correct information from it and remove the unessential information then system performance will increase.

In future we have to identify the unusual information that mislead the system and try to remove this kind of noise from the question. In future, we will try to port our system in other domains like news, business intelligence etc. Also there is no good evaluation system to evaluate the performance of question answering system, so in future we would have planned to design automated evaluation scheme to evaluate the performance of question answering system.

Acknowledgments

The work has been carried out with support from Indo - French Centre for the Promotion of Advanced Research (IFCPAR) funded Project "An Advanced platform for question answering systems" (Project No. 4200-IT-1).

References

Carol Friedman. 1989. A General Computational Treatment of the Comparative. In Proceedings of the 27th Annual Meeting of the ACL.

C. Kennedy, K. Allen. 2006. Comparatives, Semantics of Lexical and Logical Semantics; Encyclopedia of Language and Linguistics, 2nd Edition, Elsevier, Oxford.

D. Olawsky. 1989. The Lexical Semantics of Comparative Expressions in a Multi-level Semantic Processor, in Proceedings of the 27th Annual Meeting on ACL, USA.

John Burger, Claire Cardie, Vinay Chaudhri, Robert Gaizauskas, Sanda Harabagiu, David Israel, Christian Jacquemin, Chin-Yew Lin, Steve Maiorano, George Miller, Dan Moldovan, Bill Ogden, John Prager, Ellen Riloff, Amit Singhal, Rohini Shrihari, Tomek Strzalkowski, Ellen Voorhees, Ralph Weishede. 2009. Issues, Tasks and Program Structures to Roadmap Research in Question & Answering. [Online] http://www.inf.ed.ac.uk/teaching/courses/tts/papers/qa_roadmap.pdf

Josef Ruppenhofer, et al. 2006. FrameNet II: Extended Theory and Practice. [Online] http://framenet.icsi.berkeley.edu/book/book.pdf

Nathalie Rose T. Lim, Patrice Saint -Dizier, Brigitte Gay, R.E. Roxas, 2009. A Preliminary Study of Comparative and Evaluative Questions for Business Intelligence. International Symposium on Natural Language Processing (IEEE-SNLP), Bangkok.

Patrick Saint-Dizier, R. Roxas, & Nathalie Rose T. Lim. 2009. Some Challenges in the Design of Comparative and Evaluative Question Answering Systems. ACL-KRAQ workshop, Singapore.

Richard J. Cooper, S.M. Ruger. 2000. A simple Question Answering System. In Proceedings of Text Retrieval Conference (TREC, Gaithersburg, MD), NIST 500-249, pp 249–255.

A Semantic Based Question Answering System for Thailand Tourism Information

Alisa Kongthon, Sarawoot Kongyoung,
Choochart Haruechaiyasak and **Pornpimon Palingoon**
Human Language Technology Laboratory (HLT)
National Electronics and Computer Technology Center (NECTEC)
Thailand Science Park, Klong Luang, Pathumthani 12120, Thailand
alisa.kon@nectec.or.th, sarawoot.kon@nectec.or.th
choochart.har@nectec.or.th, pornpimon.pal@nectec.or.th

Abstract

This paper reports our ongoing research work to create a semantic based question answering system for Thailand tourism information. Our proposed system focuses on mapping expressions in Thai natural language into ontology query language (SPARQL).

Topic: Language processing, reasoning aspects

1 Introduction

The Semantic Web can provide significant impact on an information intensive industry such as tourism where information plays an important role for decision and action making. Tourism is one of the economic factors in Thailand. From the statistics provided by the Office of Tourism Development[1], the number of tourists visiting Thailand in 2010 is approximately 16 millions. Providing an automatic question-answering system on tourism information would be very useful for tourists to plan their trips.

In this paper, we propose a semantic based question answering system for Thailand tourism information. Our proposed system focuses on converting expressions in Thai natural language into SPARQL[2], an ontology query language.

Currently there already exist publicly available formal tourism ontologies. Notable ones include Harmonise Ontology (Fodor and Werthner, 2005), Mondeca Tourism Ontology[3], OnTour Ontology[4] and TAGA Travel Ontology[5]. These ontologies are designed to integrate and manage heterogeneous tourism data (Prantner et al., 2007). In our proposed system, we apply publicly available OnTour Ontology to represent the tourism concepts and relations such as place, accommodation, restaurant and attraction.

There are also number of studies that provide natural language interfaces to ontologies. Notable works include ORAKEL (Cimiano et al., 2007), NLP-Reduce (Kaufmann et al., 2007), PANTO (Wang et al., 2007), AquaLog (Lopez et al., 2007), QuestIO (Damljanovic et al., 2008) and FREyA (Damljanovic et al., 2010). However, these approaches only focus on English language query. Since Thai language characteristics are different than English, we propose an approach to map expressions in Thai natural language to ontology based on pattern analysis.

2 The Proposed System

The proposed system is illustrated in Figure 1. The information is collected, by using a crawler, from various websites related to tourism in Thailand. We collect two different types of information. The first type is general information such as places to visit, accommodations, attractions, and restaurants which are used to design our tourism (named *Tour*) ontology. The second type is requests or questions for tourism information posted on public discussion forums. These natural language requests are used to construct a tourism related lexicon and an annotated corpus for request pattern analysis.

[1] The office of Tourism Development, *http://www.tourism.go.th*

[2] SPARQL Query Language for RDF, *http://www.w3.org/TR/rdf-sparql-query/*

[3] Mondeca Tourism Ontology, *http://www.mondeca.com*

[4] DERI, OnTour Ontology, *http://e-tourism.deri.at/ont/index.html*

[5] TAGA Ontology, *http://taga.sourceforge.net/owl/index.html*

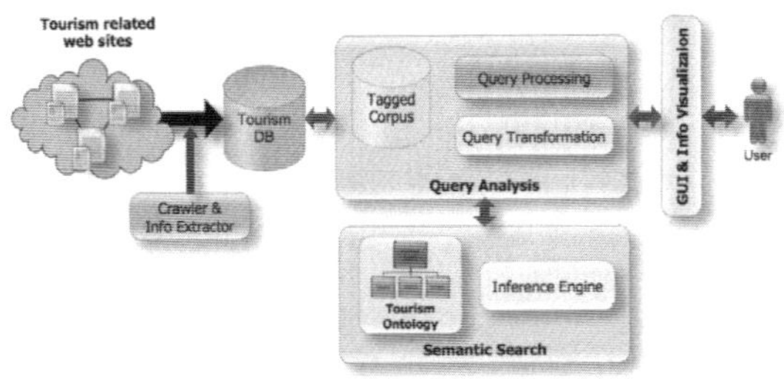

Figure 1. The proposed system

The performance of our proposed system depends on the design and completeness of the lexicon. We distinguish lexicon into two types: domain-dependent and domain-independent. For the domain of tourism, the domain-dependent lexicons could be, for instance, "place," "accommodation," "restaurant," "attraction," and "price". The domain-independent lexicon consists of regular words, which provide different functions in the sentence. For our proposed system, we design two different domain-independent lexicons as follows:

- **Particles (Par)**: In Thai language refer to the sentence endings which are normally used to add politeness of the speakers (Cooke, 1992). Examples are ครับ (Krub) and ค่ะ (Ka).

- **Request (Req)**: Phrases that are used for request information. Example is ช่วยแนะนำ (could you suggest).

The collected natural language requests or questions are first manually annotated according to the domain-dependent and domain-independent tag sets. From this tagged corpus, we can construct request patterns by collecting text segments, which contain both domain-dependent and domain-independent words.

Given a user query of natural language request, the query analysis module starts by performing the word segmentation. Some of the tokenized words with their variations or similar meanings will be normalized into a standard term. The next step is to construct patterns from these processed natural language requests. These patterns will be converted into SPARQL, which is then used to query our *Tour* ontology located in the semantic search module. Figure 2 shows an example of our *Tour* ontology and a partial instantiation of an accommodation. The ontology consists of seven different classes: *Accommodation, Restaurant, Attraction, Type, Cost, Address,* and *GPSCoordinates*. Each class contains different properties. For instance, the Accommodation class contains "hasName," "hasType," "hasMaxPeople," "hasCost," and "hasGPSCoordinates" properties. Inference engine is also used to derive new knowledge. For instance, when a user requests for an accommodation, some nearby restaurants can also be recommended to him/her.

3 An Illustrative Case: Accommodation Information Request

To evaluate the proposed system, we perform an experiment with an illustrative case on accommodation information request.

3.1 Corpus Preparation

We collected 300 natural language requests on accommodation from *Pantip.com*, one of the famous Thai language discussion forums. Table 1 shows the lexicon related to accommodation request.

Type	Examples
Accommodation Clue <Acc_Clue>	ที่พัก (accommodation), ที่นอน (sleeping place)
Accommodation Type <Acc_Type>	โรงแรม (hotel), รีสอร์ท (resort), โฮมสเตย์ (homestay)
Accommodation Condition <Acc_Cond>	หมาเข้าได้ (dogs allowed), มีสระว่ายน้ำ (have swimming pool)
Place <Place>	กรุงเทพ (Bangkok), เชียงใหม่ (Chiangmai), หัวหิน (Hua Hin)
Location Clue <Loc_Clue>	ที่ (at), บน (on), ใกล้ (near), แถวๆ (not far from)
Price Clue <Price_Clue>	ราคา (price), ค่าที่พัก (accommodation price)
Price Condition <Price_Cond>	ถูก (cheap), ไม่แพง (not expensive), กำลังดี (moderate)
People Clue <Ppl_Clue>	ไปกัน (going with), มากัน (coming with), มีทั้งหมด (total number of)
Unit <Unit>	คน (person), บาท (Baht)

Table 1. Lexicon related to accommodation

3.2 Experiments

To verify if our lexicon is sufficient in identifying accommodation request, we first perform request identification task. This task aims to distinguish between requests for accommodation

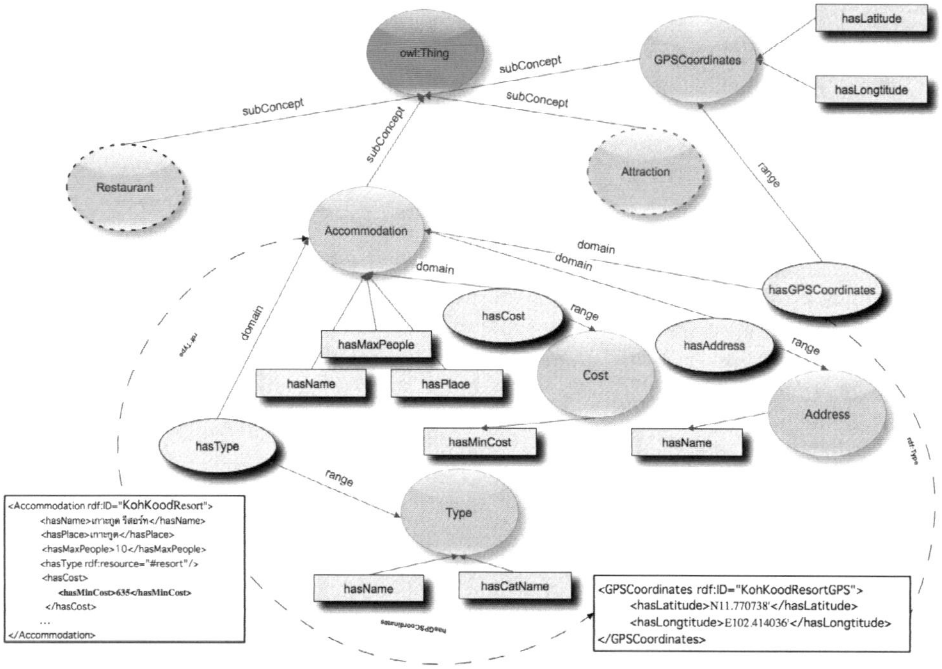

Figure 2. An example of *Tour* ontology

and any other types of requests or questions. We initially performed evaluation on 600 questions where 300 are accommodation requests and other 300 are not. The identification result yields 89% recall and 95% precision.

We then use the tagged corpus and the extracted lexicon to construct the most frequently occurred patterns. For our 300 accommodation requests, the total number of extracted patterns is 168. Table 2 shows some examples of the top-5 accommodation request patterns. These patterns are then converted into SPARQL queries. The following example (Example 1) illustrates the conversion from natural language requests to SPARQL queries. The given request asks for recommended accommodations with a constraint on the number of people staying.

Example 1:

Natural language request input:
รบกวนแนะนำที่พักที่เกาะกูดหน่อยครับ ไปกัน 10 คน
Could you suggest accommodation at Koh Kood "noi krub?", going with 10 people

Word segmentation process:
รบกวนแนะนำ|ที่พัก|ที่|เกาะกูด|หน่อย|ครับ| |ไปกัน| |10| |คน|

Pattern construction process:
รบกวนแนะนำ<Req>|ที่พัก<Acc_Clue>| |ที่<Loc_Clue>|เกาะกูด<Place>| |หน่อย<Par> |ครับ<Par>| |ไปกัน<Ppl_Clue>| |10<Number>| |คน<Unit>|

Extracted pattern:
<Req> <Acc_Clue> <Loc_Clue> <Place> <Ppl_Clue> <Number><Unit>

SPARQL conversion:

```
SELECT ?a WHERE
  {
  tour:Tourist   tour:hasAccomodation ?a.
  {{?a       tour:hasPlace "เกาะกูด".}
  UNION { ?a    tour:hasAddress ?a.
     ?b   tour:hasName "เกาะกูด". }}
  ?a       tour:hasMaxPeople "10"
  }
```

No.	Top-5 accommodation request patterns
1	**<Req> <Acc_Clue> <Loc_Clue> <Place>** <ช่วยเลือก> <ที่พัก> <ที่> <พัทยา> <Please help select> <accommodation> <in> <Pattaya>
2	**<Req> <Acc_Clue> <Place>** <แนะนำ> <ที่พัก> <หาดป่าตอง> <Suggest> <accommodation> <Patong Beach>
3	**<Req> <Acc_Type> <Loc_Clue> <Place>** <รบกวนแนะนำ> <โฮมสเตย์> <ใกล้> <ตลาดน้ำอัมพวา> <Please suggest> <homestay> <near> <Amphawa floating market>
4	**<Req> <Acc_Clue> <Loc_Clue> <Place> <Acc_Cond>** <ช่วยแนะนำ> <ที่นอน> <แถวๆ> <หัวหิน> <มีสระว่ายน้ำใหญ่ๆ> <Please suggest> <sleeping place><near> <Hua Hin> <having a large swimming pool>
5	**<Req> <Acc_Clue> <Place> <Acc_Cond>** <แนะนำ> <ที่พัก> <เขาใหญ่> <เอาน้องหมาไปได้> <Suggest> <accommodation> <Khao Yai> <dogs allowed>

Table 2. Top-5 accommodation request patterns with examples

The derived SPARQL will be used to query our *Tour* ontology. For instance, our system will select "Koh Kood Resort" (as shown in the instantiation in Figure 2) as one of the recommended accommodations for the request in Example 1.

3.3 Discussion

Our experiment shows that most words from the lexicon related to accommodations can be derived and mapped into relevant structure in our *Tour* ontology. However, some content, especially those belong to accommodation condition (i.e., <Acc_Cond>), are difficult to extract since the ways to explain conditions can be much varied and very descriptive. Table 3 shows some examples of challenging cases for accommodation condition.

No.	Some difficult cases for "accommodation condition"
1	นั่งรถประจำทางไปเที่ยวสะดวก (convenient to take the bus)
2	ใกล้กับงานแห่เทียน (closer to the Candle Festival)
3	เหมาะสำหรับจัดกิจกรรมรับน้อง (suitable for holding a college orientation activity)
4	เน้นกินเหล้า สังสรรค์ (focus on drinking and partying)
5	มีรถมอเตอร์ไซด์เช่าแถวสนามบิน (have motorcycle rental service near the airport)

Table 3. Examples of difficult cases for "accommodation condition"

Some of these conditions would require an inference engine to help identify the answer. For example, in Case No.2, the distance between each retrieved accommodation and attraction (i.e., the Candle Festival in this case) will be calculated based on their GPS coordinates. Only the accommodations located near the Candle Festival will be recommended to the user. In addition, some rule base can be applied in order to transform descriptive language into more structured format.

4 Conclusion and future work

In this paper, we proposed a framework for a semantic question-answering system for Thailand tourism information. Our proposed system focuses on mapping expressions in Thai natural language into ontology query language (SPARQL). The proposed method first constructs a set of patterns from a tagged corpus containing both domain-dependent and domain-independent lexicons. The derived patterns are then converted into relevant SPARQL queries. We performed an experiment on a case study regarding accommodation information requests. Our experiment results showed that some features such as place, accommodation type, price, and number of people staying can be extracted from the natural language query and easily converted into corresponding SPARQL queries. However, in some cases such as the description of accommodation condition are more difficult to extract. For future work, we plan to apply some rule base and inference engine to help derive answers to the user.

References

Cimiano P., Haase P. and Heizmann P. 2007. Porting natural language interfaces between domains: an experimental user study with the orakel system. *Proc. of the 12th International Conference on Intelligent User Interface*. 180-189.

Cooke, J.R. 1992. Thai Sentence Particles: Putting the Puzzle Together. *Proc. of the Third International Symposium on Language and Linguistics*, 1105-1119.

Damljanovic D., Tablan V. and Bontcheva K. 2008. A text-based query interface to owl ontologies. *In 6th Language Resources and Evaluation Conference (LREC)*.

Damljanovic D., Agatonovic M. and Cunningham H. 2010. Natural language interfaces to ontologies: combining syntactic analysis and ontology-based lookup through the user interaction. *The Semantic Web: Research and Application*. 106-120.

Fodor O. and Werthner H. 2005. Harmonise: A Step Toward and Interoperable E-Tourism Marketplace. *International Journal of Electronic Commerce*, 11-39.

Kaufmann E., Bernstein A. and Fischer L. 2007. NLP-Reduce: A naïve but domain-independent natural language interface for querying ontologies. *Proc. of the European Semantic Web Conference*.

Lopez V., Uren V., Motta E. and Pasin M. 2007. Aqualog: An ontology-driven question answering system for organizational semantic intranets. *Web Semantics: Science, Services and Agents on the World Wide Web*. 5(2), 72-105.

Prantner K., Ding Y., Luger M., Yan Z. and Herzog C. 2007. Tourism Ontology and Semantic Management System: State-of-the-arts Analysis. *IADIS International Conference WWW/Internet 2007*. 111-115.

Wang C., Xiong M., Zhou Q. and Yu Y. 2007. Panto: A portable natural language interface to ontologies. *The Semantic Web: Research and Application*.473-487.

AUTHOR INDEX